Laissez les Bons Temps Rouler

"Let the Good Times Roll"

Laissez les Bons Temps Rouler is written by Tim Hall

Published and printed by:
    Lifevest Publishing
    4901 E. Dry Creek Rd., #170
    Centennial, CO 80122
    www.lifevestpublishing.com

        Printed in the United States of America

            ISBN 978-1-59879-326-8

To Miss Elleen,
Mom,
who started all of this way back when.

To Carol,
my wonderful wife of 40 years...
Wow...can you believe 40 years...

and to Sigried, Brett and Brandon,
my first and still my favorite taste testers.

Table of Contents

Laissez les Bon Temps Rouler

I've been cooking seriously most of my life and have thought for some time that I should assemble all the recipes I've collected over the last forty plus years and put them together in a cookbook. As the project evolved, it became apparent that this book has as much to do with the stories about the recipes as it does the recipes. To tell the truth, many of the anecdotes are a recounting of a good time we had when some friends gathered to eat. In the culture in which I grew up, gatherings with family and friends, cooking and eating are all part of the social fabric. I hold the view that life is a celebration best shared with others, and my wife, Carol, and I have made a lifelong pursuit of it. The old familiar Cajun phrase, *"Laissez les Bon Temps Rouler" (let the good times roll),* has never held truer than in our household. Over the years we have hosted countless dinner parties during which we have fed literally hundreds of people using these recipes.

Some of my earliest recollections involve me in the kitchen. When I was very young, my mother ran a restaurant and catering service in Marksville, Louisiana. Mom was a great cook and introduced us all to a wonderful world of tastes that set a level of expectation that has had a lifelong impact. I was never too far from the kitchen when I was growing up, and that has been the case all my life.

My first experience in cooking began when I joined a Boy Scout Troop and discovered that there was a merit badge for campfire cookery. My oldest best friend since the first grade, Bobby DeLaune, and I decided we were going to get that badge. In order to practice for this undertaking we used to hike two or three miles up the Red River from our house and spend the day playing in the woods along the banks just past the old railroad trestle. To be honest we spent most of our time preparing elaborate campfire meals and eating. We would leave early in the morning so we could cook breakfast as well. Over the years I've tried a few times to fix a scrambled egg sandwich with fried bologna that tasted as good as those on the riverbank and I've never duplicated it. I believe sand is the missing ingredient.

Once when we arrived at our customary campsite we found a hobo camped there! If memory serves me, we were scared to death until he reassured us that he meant no harm. Once we were convinced of that, we set about cooking our meal and fed that hobo like he hadn't been fed in a while. He ate that way too! From then on we always brought extra food on our Saturday hikes anticipating any "guests" that might show up. As I recall it, there was only one other occasion when we had a visitor, but we usually managed to eat the extra rations ourselves. On our hikes home we often picked dewberries when they were in season and brought them to Bobby's house where his mother would make us a delicious cobbler. I don't remember when we made our last sortie up the river; it must have been sometime around the end of the eighth grade, but those memories are among my most cherished. A good friend and good food...it was the start of what was to become a lifelong trend.

Carol and I got married in September 1966 at the start of our senior year in college. For the next two years, and in truth, to this day, we had a very close association with my former roommate, Billy Ray Stokes and his beautiful wife, Beverly. We have eaten many meals together but none more memorable than the lasagna that Carol cooked one night in Ruston, Louisiana. To complete the mood we had a small glass sided lantern with a candle in it. When suspended over the table, the lantern turned slowly in the airflow generated by the hurricane force air conditioner in the front window. That lighting together with music provided by the sound track from Rome Adventure created what we thought was a very romantic atmosphere. We still enjoy that memory.

After finishing college in 1968, I was employed by South Central Bell and moved to Baton Rouge,Louisiana. Once Carol, our new baby daughter, Sigried, and I were settled in our apartment, I got the urge to have biscuits for breakfast one Saturday morning. It was then that I realized I didn't have a clue as to how to bake biscuits. I well remembered what they should taste like and I set about experimenting with several combinations over the next few weeks. After some trial and error (and some hockey puck results) I finally found the right mix and wrote it down. That was in 1968 and that recipe has been responsible for at least a dozen boxcar loads of biscuits in my home since then. I don't know why I didn't call my number one resource, Mom, for her secret (a regular occurrence in later years), but when we compared recipes sometime later they were almost exactly the same. That was my first recipe...Tim's Never Fail, Lighter-Than-Air Buttermilk Biscuits. I was so proud of those biscuits that I used to bake them for everyone at the office. There are several people from my first office that I regularly correspond with, and they still talk about those biscuits! As a matter of fact, throughout my career, I brought hot biscuits to the office and always had the same reaction.

I was only in Baton Rouge that first time a few months before being transferred to Lake Charles, Louisiana and another department. Shortly after my arrival, all employees in the Lake Charles district were invited to a gumbo on Friday evening in one of the parks near the lake. Several of the men in the company got together in the early afternoon to prepare the gumbo and I was invited along to help. These fellows went about the task with a wonderful finesse and they had a great time while they worked. There were about 300 people that attended this affair and a half a dozen men prepared the whole meal! It was a great chicken and sausage gumbo and everybody had a good time. There was an obvious level of esprit de corps in this large group of people that worked together. A lot of walls are broken down when people get together and eat a great meal. I saw it that night and I've never forgotten it. I've been hooked ever since.

Over the next several years I began to cook at every opportunity. Carol and I would invite people over to visit and I would cook for the group. As the groups got bigger, I experimented with larger proportions. It was all great fun and the celebrations just got bigger and better.

One meal that I specifically recall from those early days took place after my old friend Bobby, his wife Sandra, Carol and I had gone crabbing south of Lake Charles in the brackish waters near the Intracoastal Canal. We caught thirteen dozen blue crabs that day. We boiled them all and ate until we could eat no more. After the meal we sat at the table and picked the meat from the crabs that were left. The next night Bobby and Sandra came over for dinner, and I made a gumbo with about 10 pounds of lump crabmeat in it that I can still taste today! At somewhere around $17.00 a pound for lump crabmeat, I'm not sure I could afford the crabmeat today, but it's a nice meal to remember.

While living in the Lake Charles area, we built a house in Sulphur, Louisiana. It was a new subdivision and ours was the second home to be built. Without knowing it we had bought a lot next door to some old classmates of ours from college. It was a fun neighborhood. Everybody was about the same age with small children. As people would move in I would go up and down the street to see what everybody was willing to throw into the pot. When I had gathered all the provisions, I would go home and cook for everybody in the neighborhood, and we would have a party at our house to welcome the new family. We made a lot of good friends that way.

A few years later, after a short stint in New Orleans, we moved to Lafayette, the center of Cajun culture in Louisiana. What a great place to live! Restaurants abounded and they were all good. Cajun specialties like crawfish, boudin, tasso, stuffed pork chops and andouille were readily available all over town. In a very short period of time we became quite spoiled. We had a lot of friends in Lafayette. Carol's brother Kenneth and his family lived there. Another couple, Bob and Patsy Campbell, old friends from Carol's hometown, had been in Lafayette for quite a while before we arrived. My old friend from childhood, Charlie Armand, was living and working in the area as well. Charlie was always looking for a little diversion from his bachelor diet of Beanie Weenies! I worked with Robert Burgess and we became fast friends. To this day we talk no less than every other week. Robert and his wife Juliet were regulars at our table. It was a great time with a lot of good friends.

In the next few years we were transferred to Birmingham, Alabama, then back to Baton Rouge. It was while in Baton Rouge the second time that we met Doug and Sara Hoeppner. Sara is a wonderfully talented artist and Doug is an equally talented engineer. Need I say more? Doug didn't cook much when we met, but after we got together and I cooked a few meals he got passionately involved in it. Doug never does anything halfway and he didn't start here. He cooks some wonderful dishes and is very adventurous in the kitchen (you had to be in a kitchen that Sara decorated). There was a pot rack hanging so low over the stove that I regularly hit my head on it when I cooked at their house. As best I can recall, those were the only times I ever wore a hard hat while cooking a gumbo! In 1979 I changed jobs and began to travel all of South Louisiana. What a wonderful opportunity to sample the Cajun culture firsthand. The people were great and the food was fabulous. There was constant inspiration to improve what we cooked and how we cooked it. We later moved back to Lake Charles and subsequently to Baton Rouge for the third time. All along the way, the trend of entertaining and making new friends continued, and in fact became a very important part of our lives.

I suppose it should not have come as a surprise that we would be drawn into fundraising activities for the children's schools from time to time. The schools were always looking for someone to cook for these events. I once cooked a seafood gumbo for 250 people to raise money for the school library. To my delight, both the gumbo and the fundraiser were a great success. The afternoon I cooked red beans and rice for everybody who attended one of the home football games in high school was one to remember. That was a lot of red beans! Once, I volunteered to cook a few quarts of gumbo for a frozen food sale to raise money for a new weight room. Before anybody knew what happened, the ladies taking orders had sold 80 quarts of chicken and sausage gumbo! That's 20 gallons! Normally it wouldn't have been a big issue but I had to be 100 miles away at eight o'clock the next morning to start a new job! Twenty gallons of gumbo cooked solo takes some time. I never heard how much they made on that fundraiser but I hope they did well!

We made a job transfer to LaCrosse, Wisconsin in November of 1989. Following that old trend we have entertained several hundred people at our home since we moved into a log cabin in the country in September 1990. To accommodate our long time avocation, we built a three-story garage with one whole floor, 768 square feet, dedicated to entertainment. We have hosted countless parties in that room, including three rehearsal dinners and one wedding, not to mention several anniversary parties and more meals auctioned for charity than I can recall. When Sigried and Mark were married both the wedding and the reception were held there. One of the three rehearsal dinners was for Kevin and Becky Murphy, two young friends and classmates of our son Brandon. Later, we hosted a rehearsal dinner for Brandon and his wife Abby. The third rehearsal dinner was for Derek and Nikki Leach, son and daughter-in-law of our good friends Ed and Linda Leach. Nikki designed the cover for this book. For two of the rehearsal dinners we seated and served 42 and 50 people respectively! For the third one folks were all over the place! Our annual anniversary party invitee list normally exceeds 100 people, and nobody misses it!

During this time we have met more people and established more lasting friendships than we can count. For Brandon's rehearsal dinner, five couples, dear friends all, would have it no other way but that they act as Wine Steward, Maitre D', wait staff and kitchen crew. Over the years we have shared a passion for good food and good company with Buz Hoefer and Marion Stuart (they are married, but she is a woman of the New Millennium and has kept her name), Ed and Linda Leach, Frank and Martha Roldan, Chris and Karen Sepich, and Dan and Judy Thelen. The wonderful meals and the good times are probably subjects for another book. It would be about Mes Amis!

Our marriage has been blessed in many ways, but most particularly with three wonderful children. As mentioned earlier our oldest child and only daughter Sigried was born in 1968 in Ruston, Louisiana. In 1972 our son Brett was born in Lake Charles, Louisiana, and while we were in Birmingham, Alabama in 1976, our third child and second son Brandon was born. All three of our children have grown up in a household where there has always been plenty of laughter, lots of good friends and good food. To them entertaining is a way of life. I once heard a Cajun humorist, Dave Petitjean, explain in his closing remarks that a central theme in the Cajun culture is to love life. He concluded by saying that those who do, often find that life loves them in return. I believe that to be a true statement. One of the greatest wishes that Carol and I have for our children is that the legacy of good friends and good food bless their households as it has ours over the years.

Laissez les bon temps rouler!

Tim, Dan and Mark serving it up

Celebration Catering LLC

As we were nearing the time when I would be able to retire, Carol and I read many articles about the difficulties people have at retirement. How one adjusts to the replacement of a lifetime routine of work and work related activities, seems to be a common problem for a lot of people. We didn't feel we would have those concerns since we both had avocations we were passionate about. Her gardening pastime had evolved into gardening fulltime, and I looked forward to finally having time to follow up on the compilation of this book. It seemed like we were set to make the jump into retirement. Well, here's what happened.

Following my retirement in February 2000, and just shortly after Brandon had graduated from UW-LaCrosse, the two of us began talking about going into the catering business. It seemed to be a logical evolution – since we had spent so many years developing recipes to serve more and more people and had studied and practiced the art of entertaining people comfortably. To make a long story short, Celebration Catering LLC opened for business in May 2000. Brandon had some time to dedicate to the project before he had to get serious about long-term commitments to career and marriage so we went after it full tilt. We would cook for anybody just about anytime and just about anywhere.

Had we been able to get the business financially productive enough to support Brandon and his wife, Abby, and the family they were starting, we might still be in the business.

It's probably best that we didn't reach that milestone because catering is one of the hardest and most demanding pursuits I've ever experienced! Following a profile that is common among caterers in South Louisiana, we cooked on the customer's premises. The idea sounds great and can be a lot of fun. Most often in Louisiana, a part of the world where cooking and eating at all sorts of functions is part of the social fabric, the on-site catering service becomes part of the party. Good caterers in Louisiana are known as much for their flair for public presentation as they are for their food. That all sounded like it was right up our alley, and it was. The downside was the amount of physical labor involved. To cater this way required loading all of the cooking equipment in a trailer, or trailers, and transporting it to the site, setting up, cooking, serving, breaking down, loading up and going back to the banquet hall to clean and store everything. All of that was in addition to prepping all of the dishes to be cooked beforehand so we had only to cook and serve on the premises. Long days and long evenings and nights were de rigueur. The business was inherently stressful, tiring and loaded with an incredible amount of detail. The minutiae involved in running the business (most of which Brandon handled) were myriad, and the challenges involved in the preparation and serving of large amounts of food could be just as daunting. Brandon and I have a good relationship but there were some times during this adventure when it certainly was tested. I love him dearly and am delighted there are no lasting scars from the experience.

It must be said that while Brandon and I ran the business, we had some unbelievable help from several dear friends and family. Interestingly enough, while we were in Louisiana on a research trip, we met a number of caterers who were kind enough to spend some time with us. One in particular made an off-handed comment that if you're in the catering business you can't have enough family and friends. It didn't take long before we came to know what he meant. Carol and Abby both were intimately involved in our great experiment. Early on, they were involved to a great degree rounding up last minute items we forgot. They also figured heavily in our Friday night Southern Style Fish Fry. Also, Sigried was a great hostess and cashier at the Friday night fish fry. My son-in-law, Mark, and good friends, Dan Thelen and Buz Hoefer ,did yeoman's work for us anytime we got in a pinch, which was quite often. They were proficient prep guys and good cooks all, and helped Brandon and me, and later just me, more times than I can recall. There were a few occasions when they complained about wages, and I dutifully doubled their hourly rate! It was the least I could do.

On many occasions we all felt like we were doing something similar to missionary work since our catering menu was primarily Louisiana cuisine. Virtually everybody we served in the LaCrosse area labored under the same timeworn Mid-Western misconception... Cajun food is too HOT! It got to the point we could almost predict the timing of that worn out pronouncement and we got sick of hearing it. By the end of 2004 I was just about ready to choke somebody! We had a lot of outstanding highs and a few real lows, but I've got to say, in our final analysis, we counted the business a success. There are now a lot of people in the area who have experienced excellent, well-prepared Louisiana cuisine. Those who ventured to try our offerings got over the "It's too hot!" syndrome and found out what real Cajun food was all about. I have fond memories of our considerable successes, and, from the vantage point of no longer being in the business, I have no need to remember the situations I didn't like.

All of this is to explain that many times in this book I will mention a certain recipe was used in the catering business. Be assured if it was used there, it's good, it can be duplicated easily and it was served to a lot of people who liked it. All in all, these are some pretty compelling reasons to try one of those recipes out.

Additionally, there was a huge benefit derived from four good years in this business that was not obvious at first. I realized when regularly preparing food for large groups of people, it becomes necessary to develop prep techniques and skills that aren't normally associated with cooking in the home. Arguably, one of the most important aspects of cooking is organization. The act of pre-measuring and arranging the ingredients in sequence of usage, known in kitchen parlance as mise en place, is a great time saver. The use of scales, timers and thermometers works well to make you more efficient and certainly improves your odds in turning out a top-notch product. Cleaning as you cook is also a good idea that more fully utilizes your kitchen space and just generally makes the cooking process more productive. The idea of putting together a recipe and then turning around to look at counters full of various utensils that need to be cleaned ruins the whole experience for me. From the standpoint of cross contamination, you eliminate a lot of potential food handling hazards by cleaning as you cook as well. Wherever feasible, I've tried to organize these recipes logically to allow for these facets of cooking.

And finally, enjoy your time in the kitchen. It is an outlet that allows lots of opportunity for creativity and experimentation. To be sure, I am not aware of a more satisfying way to spend a leisurely Saturday afternoon than preparing a well cooked and tastefully served meal for some good friends.

Let's celebrate by cooking up a great meal!

Brandon and Dan at Turkey Fest,
where we fried 93 turkeys one day

Let The Good Times Begin

As far back as I can remember, breakfast has always been one of my favorite meals. It just seems that the smells and tastes of breakfast are in a class of their own. What smells better than bacon frying in the morning, and is there anything that beats some really good Buttermilk Pancakes with a side of spicy breakfast sausage? Yeah, there is, a hot bowl of Mom's Cush-Cush and Café au Lait. You may still have a bad day, but there is no reason not to start it off right!

As our children were growing up we often had great breakfasts on the weekend when I had time to cook. Those were special times and I always loved to cook for the group and they always seemed to love eating it. I just didn't feel right letting them start out on a Saturday without a great breakfast. Some of my all-time favorite recipes are included in this section, and you can believe they are time worn with very high approval ratings.

Additionally, over the years we have served many brunches that included a variety of these recipes.

18 ~ Tim's Never Fail Lighter Than Air Buttermilk Biscuits

20 ~ Sweet Potato Biscuits

21 ~ Tim's Incomparable Buttermilk Pancakes

22 ~ Buttermilk Aebleskivers

24 ~ Belgian Waffles

25 ~ Buttermilk Waffles

26 ~ Unbelievable Baked Apple Pancakes

27 ~ Cornmeal Pancakes

28 ~ New Orleans French Market Beignets

29 ~ Great Granola

30 ~ Cush-Cush and Café au Lait

32 ~ Pure Pork Breakfast Sausage

33 ~ Sausage and Egg Soufflé

34 ~ Cheesy Hash Browns

Tim's Never-Fail, Lighter Than Air Buttermilk Biscuits

As recounted in the preface of this book, my biscuit recipe was the first one I worked on back in 1968. Just like breakfast is a favorite meal, biscuits are a favorite part of it. Working out this recipe all those years ago was a matter of necessity. There really are a few secrets to making good biscuits I learned along the way. Even though there are different schools of thought about sifting dry ingredients, I always sift them for this recipe. If nothing else it disperses the leavening agents throughout the mixture and that can't be a bad thing. I've never made this recipe satisfactorily by cutting the shortening into the flour with a pastry cutter: I've found it works best if done by hand. There is something about doing this step by hand that makes a difference. I don't know exactly what that something is, but I know it makes a difference. If you're squeamish about getting your hands dirty, you might as well understand now that it's going to be difficult to work in the kitchen! You have to handle food in order to prepare it well. Besides, warm water and soap work just fine. Go ahead and put your hand into the bowl and pick up one of the tablespoons of shortening with a handful of flour. Squeeze the shortening and flour and let it fall through your fingers. Continue this until the flour and shortening are mixed to a granular consistency. Now it's ready for the buttermilk. Secondly, it's bad form to knead biscuit dough too much because it makes the biscuits tough. The biscuits turn out best when kneaded lightly by folding the dough over onto itself about three or four times. My preference is to pat the dough into a square and then fold it in thirds for about three or four repetitions ending up with a square. Then it can be rolled out lightly and cut. And finally, I have always

2 cups flour
1 tablespoon baking powder
½ teaspoon salt
¼ teaspoon soda
4 tablespoons shortening
1 cup buttermilk

Preheat oven to 450°
Prep time: 20 minutes
Cooking time: 10 minutes
Yield: 10-12 biscuits

Sift all dry ingredients together. Mix in the shortening as described above. Add the buttermilk and with a large serving spoon work the mixture into a consistent dough ball and turn onto a floured surface. Knead as described above. When the dough is well incorporated and smooth, lightly roll it out with a rolling pin on a floured surface and cut the biscuits. If the dough is rolled out to about ½ to ¾ inch thickness the biscuits will rise sufficiently to allow you to break them apart by inserting a fork in the side. This allows you to butter them while they are still hot, a desirable move since nobody likes a pat of cold butter in a biscuit. To bake the biscuits spray a cast iron griddle with Baker's Joy and place the biscuits where they are just touching. Bake at 450° until golden brown on the top, about 10 minutes.

Tim's Never-Fail, Lighter Than Air Buttermilk Biscuits

cooked them on a cast iron griddle. It retains and spreads heat very well and makes a nice crust on the bottom of the biscuits.

There may be some critics who would argue any of these points, but I assure you I've thrown away very few uneaten biscuits in the last 40 years. It is my opinion that the success of this recipe is more about technique than it is ingredients.

Here are a few tips:

• Several times in recent years we have made gift baskets of food to give at Christmas. One item we've included is a biscuit mix that is nothing more than the dry ingredients mixed with the shortening and sealed in a Ziploc bag. We've packaged it in a neat little brown bag with a hangtag explaining how to use the mix. Add buttermilk and follow the recipe instructions. This makes a very personal gift.

• If you don't have a good cutter, an empty tin can with both ends cut out makes a great one. I've been using the same tomato can for about 20 years. Obviously the number of biscuits yielded will vary with the size of the cutter.

• I have found that this recipe expands beautifully. The only limitation I ever experienced is related to just how big of a dough ball one can handle! As I recall, I've mixed as much as 6 or 7 times this recipe at one time. When doing that, the flour was measured by weight and the other dry ingredients were whisked into the flour to disperse them throughout the mixture.

Sweet Potato Biscuits

I love biscuits. Of course, my favorite is the buttermilk biscuit recipe that I mastered way back in Baton Rouge, Louisiana. But, I've got to tell you, these biscuits are a solid second. They are outstanding with butter and some good honey. Jellies are OK, but the honey does it right. I found the recipe while rummaging around in some old cookbooks that belonged to my mother-in-law, Ruth Cook. Where the book came from and who assembled it escapes me now (I think the ladies at the First United Methodist Church in El Dorado, Arkansas published the book), but this recipe was definitely worth a save. I increased the baking powder from the original and used butter instead of margarine.

2 Cups flour
1 tablespoon baking powder
1 teaspoon salt
1 tablespoon sugar
¼ cup melted butter
¾ cup mashed cooked sweet potatoes
¾ cup buttermilk
½ teaspoon soda

Preheat the oven to 450°
Prep time: 25 min.
Cook time: 10 minutes
Yield: 10-12

Sift flour, baking powder and salt into a medium bowl.

Mix the sugar and melted butter with the sweet potatoes and beat until fluffy. Stir soda into buttermilk and blend with the sweet potato mixture. Pour the liquid mixture into the dry ingredients and stir only until moistened. Turn dough onto lightly floured surface and knead lightly until dough is soft and smooth. (See kneading technique in Tim's Never Fail Lighter Than Air Buttermilk Biscuits.) Gently roll out dough to about ½ to ¾ inch thickness. Cut biscuits and place on a lightly greased cast iron griddle and bake until golden brown, about 10 minutes. This recipe makes about 10-12 biscuits.

Tim's Incomparable Buttermilk Pancakes

Man cannot live on biscuits alone. With the addition of more children, it became necessary to expand the breakfast menu. Pancakes seemed to be a logical direction to explore because all kids like pancakes. As had happened with the original biscuit episode, I tried several different recipes over a period of time and finally settled on the following combination. I borrowed ideas from three or four different recipes, but the most effective one involves separating the eggs. Once the batter is made, you simply fold the beaten whites into the batter and it makes the pancakes "poofier." We bought one of those electric griddles that could cook eight good-sized pancakes and I couldn't keep up with three children. I took that to mean the recipe was good. Kids don't lie about food! The proof of that statement is that when any of our grandchildren spend the night they always want one of Papa's special breakfasts. Ah, yes! It warms the heart.

As a side note, the Men's Club recently used this recipe for a Sunday morning pancake breakfast at Blessed Sacrament Church. There were 208 people there that morning who found out what I already knew. These pancakes are good. If you're interested they used 6 gallons of buttermilk and nearly 25 pounds of flour, 8 dozen eggs and a bunch of butter. Do I need to tell you that this recipe expands easily with no loss of quality?

2 ½ cups flour
1 tablespoon baking powder
1 teaspoon salt
1 teaspoon soda
1 tablespoon sugar
1 egg, separated
3 cups buttermilk
1 tablespoon melted butter

Prep time: 20 min.
Cook time: Approx. 5 min. per pancake
Yield: 18

Sift all dry ingredients together. Combine the buttermilk and egg yolk in the bowl of a stand mixer. Set the mixer on medium, and using the paddle attachment, slowly add a large serving spoon of the dry mixture at a time to the liquid in the mixing bowl. When this is fully blended add the melted butter and mix well. Remove the bowl from the mixer and set aside. In a separate bowl, beat the egg white until stiff and fold into the batter with a large serving spoon. These pancakes rise on the griddle and are very thick. Cook each one until somewhat dry on the top before flipping to avoid having an underdone center. If you have some big eaters around, get a head start or you'll never get any breakfast! This recipe makes approximately eighteen 5-inch pancakes.

Buttermilk Aebleskivers

I have been collecting cast iron cookware for many years now and have managed to gather up quite a lot of it. One of the interesting aspects of collecting this type of cookware is trying to figure out the intended use of some pieces. Carol and I found one such item that looked interesting but we had no clue regarding its intended use. It is a skillet of sorts with seven rounded cups built into it. The antique store where we bought it labeled it as an egg cooker. That just didn't seem right but we bought it anyway. If nothing else it had conversational value. We looked around for some time trying to determine its origin but couldn't turn up anything. Finally we hung it on the wall where we have quite a bit of cast iron cookware displayed and forgot about it. One day a friend, Jim Murphy, was looking at the collection and he picked up the piece and asked where we had found the Aebleskiver cooker! Did we jump all over that? Jim explained that an Aebleskiver was a type of Scandinavian pancake. The aebleskivers are cooked by pre-heating the pan and melting a pat of butter in each of the cups before filling it about half full with the batter. Jim went on to say that when he and his family lived in Iowa, the church they attended used to have aebleskiver breakfasts on the weekends as fundraisers. This was all very interesting and answered a lot of our questions... now try to find a recipe for the batter! Read on.

For some time, Carol regularly attended auctions around the LaCrosse, Wisconsin area. During one such auction she bought a sort of grab bag of items just to get one thing she wanted. When she got home I was looking

3 cups flour
1 teaspoon baking powder
½ teaspoon salt
1 teaspoon soda
1 tablespoon sugar
1 egg, separated
2 ½ cups buttermilk

Prep time: 15 min.
Cook time: 5 min. per batch
Yield: 35 aebleskivers

Sift the dry ingredients together and set aside. Separate the eggs and set the whites aside. Mix the yolks and the buttermilk in the large bowl of a stand mixer. With the mixer on low speed gradually add the dry ingredients until a thick batter is formed. Remove the bowl from the mixer. With a hand-held mixer, beat the egg whites until peaks form and then fold them into the batter with a large serving spoon. Pre-heat the aebleskiver pan and add a small pat of butter in each cup. Fill each cup approximately half full with batter and cook as you would a pancake. When bubbles form on the top and the edges begin to dry, flip the aebleskiver and allow it to cook on the other side.

Here's a cooking tip. I've since read some recipes that call for placing a small piece of apple in the batter when you pour it into the cup. Cook the aebleskiver as you normally would. When done these are served dusted with powdered sugar. Very good! They work quite well with syrup or honey, too.

through the box that contained some kitchen tools and a few cook-books. Would you believe the first book I picked up was a collection of Scandinavian recipes from an old restaurant in Stoughton, Wisconsin named the Norse Chalet? Guess what was on page 39? I've since found several recipes but like this one the best. I resorted to an old technique used in the pancake and waffle recipes and separated the eggs. After the batter is made I beat the whites until stiff and fold them into the batter. It works as well here as it did in the other recipes.

There is some technique involved in flipping these little aebleskivers in the cup. As with pancakes the aebleskiver is cooked on one side until bubbles form and the uncooked top begins to dry. I use a butter spreader with a rounded tip. Push down on the edge and allow the spreader to follow the curvature of the cup. With the spreader and a fork I position the aebleskiver squarely, or should I say roundly, in the cup. Write me a letter when you master this bit of finesse!

Tim cooking in the "big pot"

Belgian Waffles

I've always liked Belgian waffles but lacked the waffle maker required to make this special treat. Carol solved that problem by giving me a Belgian waffle maker for Christmas one year. That triggered a roughly two-year search for the "right" recipe. I tried several combinations but they all failed to give me the kind of crust that I wanted. Short of a special malted waffle mix that is sold at Williams Sonoma I was stumped. While Carol and I were on a trip to New Orleans we stopped in a bookstore on Decatur Street. I was browsing in the cookbook section and found a recipe that had the look of the "right" one. I didn't want to buy the whole book for one recipe so I got a piece of scrap paper from Carol's purse and wrote down the ingredients. I would be glad to give credit to the author but I have no clue as to whom that might be! When we got home I tried the recipe and it was the one! It doesn't have the malty flavor normally associated with Belgian waffles, but it has a great crust.

1 cup flour
¾ teaspoon baking powder
¼ teaspoon salt
¼ teaspoon soda
1 teaspoon sugar
1 egg, separated
1 cup sour cream
½ cup milk
1 tablespoon melted butter

Prep time 15 min.
Cook time: 5 min. per waffle
Yield: 5

Sift all dry ingredients together. Beat the egg whites until peaks begin to form and set aside. Whisk the egg yolk, sour cream, milk and melted butter in the bowl of a stand mixer. While the mixer is on medium speed gradually add the dry ingredients until well blended. Fold in the beaten egg whites. Cook on a preheated waffle iron and top with syrup, fruit compote or fresh fruit.

Buttermilk Waffles

I really don't have a fixation on buttermilk but it seems that all of my favorite breakfast foods have buttermilk in them. It must be a Southern thing! We were given a waffle maker for Christmas one year, and I promptly set about figuring out how to make good waffles. By this time I was getting pretty good at this cooking thing so this recipe didn't take too long. Once again, I separated the eggs and reserved the whites for the last step. I also added butter to this mixture and the results were good enough that I had to buy a second waffle maker to keep up with the hungry horde. Actually, the horde was still the same three children, just a little older with bigger appetites. On those rare occasions when there was left over batter, I used to cook it up and then freeze the waffles in a Ziploc bag. It was easy for the little ones to break these apart and toast them on a weekday morning for a quick breakfast. These waffles had such a high approval rating that it became standard procedure to make extra batter.

2 cups flour
1½ teaspoons baking powder
½ teaspoon salt
¼ teaspoon soda
1 tablespoon sugar
1 egg, separated
2½ cups buttermilk
6 tablespoons melted butter

Prep time: 15 min.
Cook time: 5 min./waffle
Yield: 10 waffles

Combine all dry ingredients. In the mixing bowl of a stand mixer combine the buttermilk, egg yolks and melted butter. Turn the mixer on about medium and add the dry ingredients one serving spoon at a time until thoroughly blended. In a separate bowl beat the egg whites until stiff. Fold the beaten egg whites into the batter and cook in a preheated waffle maker. You can't miss with this one.

Unbelievable Baked Apple Pancakes

As I have mentioned before, breakfast foods are some of my favorites. I had something similar to these pancakes many years ago on a vacation trip that Carol and I had taken just prior to the birth of our youngest child, Brandon. Her parents kept the two older children and we took a trip to Washington, D. C. and the surrounding area. We were day tripping along Interstate Highway 95 that runs North-South in Virginia when I noticed a restaurant named Aunt Sarah's Pancake House! Too late! We missed the first one but I didn't miss the next one! When we sat down to eat, the waitress presented us with what was described as an award-winning menu. I didn't know what to expect but soon found out that the award was for descriptive writing! If everything on that menu tasted as good as it was written up to be this was going to be a great place to eat! We never found out if everything was that good but the apple pancakes certainly were. These were basic pancakes topped with a wonderful apple compote and whipped cream. I have to tell you here that since Carol was pregnant with Brandon she was really watching her diet. She also watched me eat these pancakes.

I didn't have a "store-bought" pancake to rival these until the summer of 1999 when Carol and I spent a few days in Chicago visiting Brandon, now a college graduate working on an internship in the big city. We ate breakfast one morning at a pancake house in downtown Chicago that specialized in baked apple pancakes. These are prepared differently than Aunt Sarah's but were certainly reminiscent of them. By the way, Carol could eat these. This version is my interpretation of what we ate in Chicago and it's pretty close.

1 cup flour
1 cup milk
4 eggs
½ teaspoon salt
¼ teaspoon nutmeg
3 apples peeled and cored and thinly sliced
½ cup butter
½ cup sugar
1 tablespoon cinnamon

Preheat oven to 400 degrees.
Prep time: 30 min.
Cook time: 25 min.
Yield: 2 pancakes

Combine flour, milk eggs, salt and nutmeg and beat two minutes until batter bubbles. It will be thick. Set aside for 5 minutes. Toss the apples in the mixture of cinnamon and sugar and sauté lightly in butter. Spoon the apples into two 9-inch pie pans that have been sprayed with Pam. Pour the batter over the apples and bake for 25 minutes. When cooled slightly place a large plate over the pan and turn it over. The caramelized cinnamon and sugar mixture and the apples will be on the top. Lightly sift powdered sugar on the top and serve. Makes two 9-inch pancakes.

Cornmeal Pancakes

I love the taste and texture of cornmeal. When we were first married someone gave us a cookbook written by Mildred Swift, a home economist featured on one of the TV stations in Monroe, Louisiana. The only recipe I remember now that came from that book was one for Cornmeal Pancakes. They were good, but the recipe was a pain and had several steps that I felt were extraneous. Many years later while foraging for another recipe in a pile of cookbooks I came across a method for making cornmeal pancakes that was a lot simpler than the one ol' Mildred had put forth back in 1966. It's easy, fast and good: three things that appeal to me. I must admit that I have a bias when it comes to these pancakes. It is the syrup. I grew up on Steen's Pure Cane Syrup from Abbeville, Louisiana. It is cooked in open kettles and is thick and dark, not too far removed from molasses. It is a great complement for these pancakes. Around our house, Steen's is often eaten with any leftover Mom's Cornbread as a dessert. That doesn't happen often since there is seldom any left over.

1 ¼ cups cornmeal (preferably
    stone ground)
¾ cup flour
1 ¾ teaspoons baking powder
¾ teaspoon salt
1 2/3 cups milk
4 tablespoons (1/4 stick) butter, melted
2 large eggs

Prep time: 20 min.
Cook time: 4 min. per pancake
Yield: 24 pancakes

Whisk together the dry ingredients and set aside. Beat the eggs in a large bowl and add the milk and melted butter. Add the dry ingredients and beat until blended. I prefer to use a stand mixer for this step, but a hand held mixer will work well. The batter will be very thin. Spoon ¼ cup of batter onto a preheated griddle and allow room for spreading. Cook as you would other pancakes. These pancakes can be held in a 200° oven until all of the pancakes are cooked and ready to serve.

This recipe makes about twenty-four 4-inch pancakes.

New Orleans French Market Beignets

Mom didn't make beignets when we were growing up. She made what she called Long de Boeufs. I don't know what that means and have no idea how she made them, but as I remember them they weren't very different from beignets. As I recall them now, Mom didn't use risen dough, which would make them very similar to the beignet mix that is sold commercially in New Orleans. Somewhere along the way Mom came up with this recipe for beignets. She told me once that my Uncle Jimmy Rabalais had procured it in New Orleans while on a business trip there. I never ascertained how he got it or if this was an original, but if it isn't it is really close to the real thing. This dough is allowed to rise overnight in the refrigerator. We catered these on several occasions for brunches but found that we had to hold an in-service training session to instruct folks in the nuances of what they were and how to eat them!

1 cup boiling water
¼ cup shortening
¼ cup sugar
1 teaspoon salt
1 cup evaporated milk
1 package yeast, dissolved in ½ cup of water
2 beaten eggs
7 ½ cups flour in all

Prep time: 30 min.
Cook time: 4 min. per batch
Yield: 36

Pour 1 cup of boiling water over mixture of ¼ cup of shortening, ¼ cup of sugar and 1 teaspoon of salt. When shortening is dissolved stir in 1 cup of evaporated milk and add the two beaten eggs. Let cool to lukewarm and add the yeast dissolved in water. Stir in 4 cups of flour and beat vigorously until mixture is smooth. Add enough flour to this batter to make soft dough (about 3-3 ½ more cups). Place in a greased bowl of sufficient size to allow the dough to rise and refrigerate until ready to use.

When ready to fry beignets, roll the dough to a ¼ inch thickness. Cut into squares using a pizza cutter and fry in very hot oil. Drain the beignets and sift powdered sugar over them. Serve hot with Café au Lait (see the recipe for Cush-Cush) and you'll feel like you're sitting at the Café du Monde in New Orleans.

Great Granola

We have made several trips to one of our favorite places, Freeport, Maine. When there, we stay at a wonderful lodging called the Harraseekeet Inn. One of the items on the breakfast buffet is an outstanding muesli. They sell it in the guest shop, at a premium I might add, and they list the ingredients on the side. I bought some on the last trip and began to experiment with the mixture when we got home. After quite a bit of reading I found that the lines between muesli and granola are somewhat blurred. Several recipes for both suggested the same ingredients and the blending of the items looked to be the same. Beginning results were somewhat lackluster, so I decided to scrap all of the recipes and make a granola that contained the things I liked and in the proportions I liked. The result has been most satisfactory. The ingredients are listed below, in groups, in the order in which they are combined.

When baked the granola will be rich golden brown and somewhat gooey. When it cools it will become crunchy and can be broken up and stored in a resealable container. I like it as a breakfast cereal with milk but it is delicious as a dry snack.

4 cups rolled oats
2 cups puffed rice
½ cup walnut pieces
½ cup slivered almonds
½ cup pecan pieces
½ cup unsalted sunflower seeds
1 package dried mixed fruit morsels
½ cup diced dried apricots
½ cup raisins
¾ cup wheat germ
½ cup brown sugar
1 tablespoon cinnamon
2 teaspoons vanilla
¾ cup honey
1 cup canola oil

Prep time: 45 min.
Cook time: 45 min.
Yield: 12 cups

Spread oats and puffed rice on a baking pan. Toast in a 350° oven for 10 minutes, stirring once. When done, pour the oats and puffed rice into a large bowl. Stir in the nuts and sunflower seeds, fruit morsels, apricots and raisins. In a separate bowl combine the honey, oil, vanilla, brown sugar, cinnamon and wheat germ and mix well. Drizzle this over the cereal mixture and blend well. The ingredients will stick together. Spread the mixture out on a large baking sheet and bake at 325° for 40 minutes. Stir the mixture at 10-minute intervals to prevent sticking and to allow it to cook evenly. Let cool and store in an airtight container. I use a 1-gallon Ziploc bag for storage. This recipe makes about 12 cups of granola.

Cush-Cush

I really need to back up here and talk about the original breakfast food in our house. I was weaned on this. As far back as I can remember Mom made cush-cush. Once you ate a bowl of cush-cush for breakfast, you were set for the day. If you were out playing and got thirsty, a glass of water would cause all that cornmeal to swell up and you forgot about being hungry! Tell me Mom didn't do that on purpose! I suppose I also need to explain that the bowls Mom used to serve my brothers and me were actually serving bowls!

I'm not really sure if this recipe originated in the Cajun culture around Marksville, Louisiana or the Native American culture from the same area. My guess is it came from both. Whatever the case, I can't sit down to a bowl of cush-cush with steaming hot café au lait and not have flashbacks.

The first secret to this recipe is to use a preheated cast iron pot and let the mixture cook until a crust forms on the bottom before breaking it up. The second secret is in the coffee.

A word about coffee is probably in order here. In Louisiana, long before I ever heard of Starbucks or any of a gazillion other brands of coffee that are now on the market, there was Community Coffee. Roasted and ground in Baton Rouge by the Saurage family for as long as I can remember and well before that, they long ago attained institution status. Community Coffee is as Louisiana as it gets. Of course you can buy light and medium roast, but I

1 cup yellow cornmeal
½ teaspoon baking powder
½ teaspoon salt
1 teaspoon sugar
½ cup milk
1 egg, beaten
Cooking oil to cover the bottom of a deep cast iron pot

Prep time: 10 min.
Cook time: 15 min.
Yield: 4 servings

Mix all dry ingredients and combine with the beaten egg and ½ cup of milk. Heat two tablespoons of hot oil in a deep cast iron pot. Pour the batter into the heated pot and allow it to cook until a crust has formed on the bottom. When a crust is formed stir the mixture and break it up. Cook the mixture on medium heat for about five to ten minutes then turn the heat off and place the top on the pot for another five minutes. This allows the cush-cush to steam and keeps it moist.

don't know where they sell it! Dark Roast Community, rich and aromatic, is a true elixir. And if you are adventurous they even have coffee with chicory. Now there's a wake up call for you! Try that with your café au lait and you'll be drinking the real deal. As information, the chicory was added during World War II when rationing was in effect. After the war it became entrenched in Louisiana culture and is now considered customary. Chicory was introduced to stretch the coffee and it did, right along with your eyelids!

milk
black coffee

In a separate saucepan scald 2-3 cups of milk. When scalded, add black coffee to taste. I use equal amounts of coffee and milk. Usually a light brownish color is just about right. Sweeten to taste. Serve the cush-cush in a deep bowl and pour the hot café au lait over it. As the Cajuns say, "Mange, cher!" Don't worry about making too much of the café au lait, you can always drink it later.

My children have eaten their share of cush-cush in their lifetime as well!

Pure Pork Breakfast Sausage

Naturally we use pure pork sausage as breakfast meat, but this recipe works well in a number of different recipes that you will find throughout the book. The inspiration for this sausage came from Veron's Meat Market, a specialty meat market in Lafayette, Louisiana. They used a pure pork sausage as a stuffing for a thick cut pork chop that was, and still is, out of this world good. It was also stuffed in a casing and in that form is incredibly good cooked on the grill. When fried in a patty it makes an outstanding breakfast sausage. We also use it as a stuffing for mushrooms with great success. This recipe as nearly approximates Veron's offering as I've been able to attain, maybe not as good, but a better than average substitute.

5 pounds coarse ground Boston butt
   or pork shoulder
1 ½ tablespoons canning (non-iodized) salt
2 tablespoons black pepper
3 tablespoons ground/rubbed sage
1 teaspoon ground coriander
2 teaspoons cayenne pepper
1 tablespoon ground thyme
1 ¼ teaspoons sugar
1 cup water.

Prep time: 15 min.
Yield: 5 pounds

Mix dry ingredients with water and then mix thoroughly with the ground pork. Chill this mixture and make into patties, which can then be frozen and used when needed. If you wish, this sausage can be stuffed in a 34mm casing or used as suggested in other recipes in this book. The yield for this recipe is five pounds of a very versatile breakfast sausage.

Sausage and Egg Soufflé

This was prepared as a breakfast entrée along with Cheesy Hash Browns for The Ladies Club at Blessed Sacrament Church in LaCrosse, Wisconsin. It's straightforward and easy to prepare ahead of time. In fact, to do it right, it should be prepared the night before and cooked the next morning. Our own Breakfast Sausage recipe works well in this dish, but Jimmy Deans' breakfast sausage is a very good substitute.

1 pound bulk pork sausage, cooked, crumbled and drained
6 slices bread, crusts removed
3 tablespoons butter
1½ cups grated Cheddar cheese
5 eggs
2 cups half and half
1 teaspoon salt
1 teaspoon dry mustard

Prep time: 10 min.
Cook time: 40-45 min.
Yield: 12 servings

Cut bread into cubes and place in a large mixing bowl. Melt butter and pour over the bread. Mix this with a large spoon until all of the bread cubes are coated with butter. Place the buttered bread cubes in a 9 X 13 inch baking dish. Sprinkle with sausage; top with cheese. Beat remaining ingredients together and pour over sausage mixture. Chill overnight. Bake uncovered at 350° for 40-45 minutes.

In the catering environment this recipe tripled will fit well in a 2½-inch full-size pan and will comfortably feed 30-32 people.

Cheesy Hash Browns

We first prepared this dish for the Ladies Club at Blessed Sacrament Church and it was an instant hit. Like several other good recipes I've found, this one was provided on the packaging of one of the ingredients, in this case the hash browns. It's amazing what one can find out by reading the packaging!

1 package (1 lb 4 oz) Simply Potatoes Shredded Hash Browns
1 can cream of mushroom soup
8 ounces shredded Cheddar cheese
¾ cup sour cream
¼ cup butter
2 tablespoons chopped onion

Prep time: 10 min.
Cook time: 45 min.
Yield: 9-12 servings

Preheat oven to 350°. Thoroughly combine all ingredients except the hash browns. Place hash browns in a large bowl and add the mixture to hash browns and stir until well mixed. Spread the mixture in a 10 X 13 inch baking dish and bake at 350° for 45 minutes. This recipe serves 9-12 people and expands easily. This is a great dish for a New Year's Day Brunch which is what we started doing after we got to the age when staying up until midnight didn't excite us anymore.

In the catering business we found that when tripling this recipe, the mixture will fit perfectly in a 2½-inch deep, full sized restaurant pan and will feed about 30 people.

Cooking at the Festival Farmer's Market

You Have to Have a Little Dough

One of my great weaknesses in life is good, hot bread. When my old friend Bobby and I were in high school, a big time soiree for us was to visit to the Holsum Bread Bakery way out on MacArthur Drive in Alexandria, Louisiana. If you went to the guard gate and gave the night watchman fifty cents, he would give you a brown paper bag. You then had to walk around to the rear door of the bakery and, once inside, back to the front where the ovens were situated. At that location the bread was coming out of the ovens on a conveyor belt with attached loaf pans on it. As the belt rolled out it would flip the fresh loaves onto another conveyor belt that ran the length of the building into a cooling room. The gentleman working in that area would pick out two hot loaves and place them in your bag. Since neither of us had a lot of money to burn, it was not unusual for us to go to one of our favorite all-night haunts called the Waddle Inn Grill and trade the waitress some hot bread for some butter and milk. You know that story has to be true because nobody could make up something like that!

Later, when my work took me all over the state, I found that all around South Louisiana there were small hometown bakeries that had been operating for many years providing great baked items for the surrounding area. In those days you could enter one of those little establishments with a couple of dollars and leave with a bag full of some of the best baked breads I've ever eaten. What a treat that was and it never failed to remind me of the old Holsum Bread Bakery.

The recipes found in this section are some of my favorite ones gleaned over a long period of years. I hope you enjoy them as much as my family and I do.

Breads

Mom's Cornbread

It is generally acknowledged that cornbread is a particularly Southern treasure. Much like gumbo, there are many variations to the recipe. I've eaten cornbread all over the South and several other states for that matter and have found only a couple that suit my taste like the one that follows. When we lived in Birmingham, Alabama there was a place downtown named John's Restaurant that cooked cornbread sticks that were outstanding. I could have made a meal on them and very nearly did every time we went there. Victor Casio, at The Chateau in Monroe, Louisiana served cornbread muffins that were very close to the same flavor and texture as Mom's Cornbread. There were some other good examples but these two stand out. I have used the following recipe to make both the cornbread sticks and muffins but find that it works best cooked as a whole cornbread in a cast iron skillet. The secret here is to preheat the shortening in the skillet on the stovetop and pour the batter into the "hot" skillet. This forms a crispy crust that has a great taste. I also have found that shortening provides a better crust than regular oil. Try it out and see what you think. The recipe expands easily and it's a good thing, because one batch is seldom enough!

¾ cup cornmeal
¼ cup flour
½ teaspoon baking powder
½ teaspoon salt
¼ teaspoon baking soda
1 teaspoon sugar
1 cup buttermilk
1 egg
1 tablespoon melted shortening in
   preheated 7- or 8-inch cast iron skillet

Preheat oven to 450º.
Prep time: 10 min.
Cook time: 20-25 min.
Yield: 8 2-inch wedges

Mix all dry ingredients. In a separate bowl, whisk the egg and add the buttermilk. Continue beating the egg and buttermilk as you add the dry ingredients. Pour the batter into the preheated 7- or 8-inch skillet and bake until golden brown. If you double it, a 10-inch skillet works well and it will produce a nice thick cornbread.

Grandmother Cook's Hot Rolls

What's better than a really good hot roll with a meal? Carol's Grandmother Cook used this recipe. We got it from Carol's cousin Patsy Berry many years ago and it has been a crowd pleaser ever since. We didn't use this recipe much in the catering business because it was too difficult, logistically, to make it along with everything we were doing. The two step rising time and the short baking time at high heat was too labor intensive to fit in with all the other tasks taking place. Most times there were only two of us in the kitchen with a lot of other things happening. I must say from a goodness standpoint our customers missed something. These rolls are light and tasty and require only light kneading. We did make ten dozen for a rehearsal dinner once and 42 people ate every one of them! I took that as a good sign.

1 package yeast
¼ cup warm water (100°)
¼ cup sugar
1 beaten egg
1 cup warm water (96° to 108°)
1½ teaspoons salt
½ cup shortening (8 tablespoons or, if you have a scale, 4 ounces)
3½ cups flour

Preheat oven to 450° after final rise
Prep time: 15 min.
Rising time: Total of 3 hours
Cook time: 9-10 min.
Yield: 3 doz. Rolls

Dissolve the yeast in ¼ cup of warm water (100°) and set aside. Beat the sugar and egg together and mix with the dissolved yeast and the salt. Add this to one cup of warm water (96° to 108°) in a large bowl. Stir this mixture and add the ½ cup of shortening. Allow the heat in the water to dissolve the shortening as much as possible and then add the flour and mix well. (Hint: You can soften the shortening in the microwave, just don't allow it to get too hot. Check the temperature before adding to the mixture.) Cover and let the dough rise until double in size. Dough rises best around 75° to 80° in an area free from drafts. This step should take about 1-1½ hours. When the dough has risen turn it out on a floured surface and lightly knead. Roll the dough out and cut to size. I normally use a two inch biscuit cutter, but a pizza cutter also works well. Place the rolls on a greased cookie sheet and cover with a dishtowel. Let rise again until doubled in bulk, about another 1-1½ hours. Preheat the oven to 450° and bake for about 9-10 minutes. When done the rolls should be a golden brown on top. This recipe yields 3 dozen two-inch rolls.

I'm fairly certain that Grandmother Cook didn't have a thermometer, scale or a microwave to work with and I would bet her rolls were just as good as these will be and possibly even better. Once you've made as many of them as she probably did, you could likely discard these tools and wing it as well.

Asphodel Bread

This bread is named for The Asphodel Plantation, which is located about 20 miles north of Baton Rouge, Louisiana. Once upon a time, a long time ago, Carol and I spent a long weekend there and thoroughly enjoyed it. The Couhig family owned it at the time, and did a fine job of restoring it and running a restaurant along with a bed and breakfast. We ate a particularly good meal there one evening and enjoyed the bread because of its unique texture and flavor. Sometime after our stay we were surprised, if not delighted, to see an article in The Baton Rouge Morning Advocate about the plantation, which included several recipes from the restaurant. The Asphodel Bread recipe was one of them. This bread is what is known as batter bread and has a wonderfully cakey texture to it. I hope you enjoy it as much as we have. The recipe originally called for Bisquick but I have found that the dry mix (including the shortening) for Tim's Never Fail Lighter- Than-Air Buttermilk Biscuits substitutes very well for the first ingredient in the recipe.

5 cups of Tim's Never Fail Lighter
  Than Air Buttermilk Biscuit Mix
4 tablespoons sugar
1 teaspoon salt
2 cups warm milk
2 tablespoons yeast (2 packets)
4 eggs
1 teaspoon cream of tartar

Prep time: 15 minutes
Rising time: Approx. 2 hrs. total
Cook time: 20-25 min.
Yield: 2 loaves

Into a very large bowl, sift the biscuit mix, sugar and salt. Soften the yeast in the warm milk. Do not heat the milk to more than 100° or it will kill the yeast. Beat the eggs with the cream of tartar and combine with the milk and yeast mixture. Pour this mixture into the dry ingredients and stir until well blended. This is a heavy, sticky batter. Set aside in a warm place covered with a damp dishtowel. When double in bulk, stir down and fill two oiled loaf pans about half full. Cover the pans and set aside until doubled in bulk again. Preheat the oven to 350°. Bake the loaves for about 20 minutes or until a cake tester inserted in the middle of one of the loaves comes out clean. These loaves freeze well; just allow them to thaw completely before reheating.

Juliet's Sour Dough Bread

I was visiting with my old friends Robert and Juliet Burgess at their home in Bossier City, Louisiana when Juliet and I got into a conversation about homemade bread. Juliet had been making really good sour dough bread for some time and offered to give me a starter. Since I had tried several times to master the art of making good bread with lackluster results, I thought this would be a good opportunity to try again so I welcomed the gift. I started right away and after about a month began to develop some facility with the process. I've often read that making good bread requires getting a "feel" for the dough and from my experience I believe that to be true. I kept at it for several months and got really good at it. The only problem that emerged was that each time I made the bread, according to the recipe, the product was three loaves. That would be three loaves about every five days. Do I need to tell you that the wonderful aroma of hot bread filled the house each time the bread was baked? Do I need to tell you that hot bread and butter is wonderful with a hot cup of coffee? Even though I began taking two loaves of fresh bread to the office on "bake day," I still had access to one whole loaf of my own. I finally had to close the bakery down because I couldn't stand the temptation anymore. My office was upset.

Sour Dough Starter

½ cup instant potatoes
2 cups warm water
½ cup sugar
2 teaspoons salt
1 package yeast

Dissolve the yeast in ½ cup of the water, add the remaining ingredients and stir well. Keep at room temperature for 24 hours, then feed with the following:

> 3 tablespoons instant potatoes
> ¾ cup sugar
> 1 cup very warm water

Mix well and add this mixture to the starter.

Let the starter stand out of the refrigerator all day or from 8-12 hours. This will not rise, it will only bubble. Stir slightly and take out one cup to make bread and return to the refrigerator. Keep the starter in the refrigerator for 3-5 days and feed again. If not making bread after feeding the starter, discard one cup. I always had a hard time discarding the cup of starter... I felt like I had to make bread with it, and that was the start of my problem with over-indulgence and bread dependency! I mean it. That's my story and I'm sticking to it!

It is necessary to feed the starter every 3-5 days but never later than 5 days. Feed it just as you did the first time with the highlighted ingredients listed. After feeding, let it stand on the counter out of the refrigerator for 8-12 hours. Stir the mixture slightly and pour out 1 cup to make bread. Return

Juliet's Sour Dough Bread

the remaining starter to the refrigerator and repeat the process every 3-5 days. You can give the one-cup of starter away as a gift to somebody else so they, too, can work on their bread dependency.

Here's a timing issue I encountered in this process. When making this bread the fermentation process is slow and it takes 12 hours for the dough to double in bulk. When you punch it down and shape it into 3 loaves the loaves have to rise another 12 hours. Unless you want to bake bread at night it's best to time the process to bake the bread in the morning, then you can eat a whole loaf by yourself and take the other two to the office for those people that never seem to have any food at home!

Sourdough Bread
Finally, we get to make bread!

6 cups bread flour
¼ cup sugar
1 tablespoon salt
1 cup Sour Dough Starter
½ cup corn oil
1½ cups warm water

Prep time: 20 min.
Total rising time: 16-24 hours
Kneading time: 30 min
Cook time: 35-40 min.

Stir together the flour, sugar and salt. Mix all ingredients in a large bowl: pat the top with oil and cover lightly with a dishtowel. Let rise in a warm place for 8-12 hours. Punch down the dough in the bowl and knead a little. Divide the dough into 3 parts and knead each part 10-15 times on a floured board or cloth. Shape the dough and place it into a greased loaf pan. Brush the loaves with oil. Cover with oiled foil or oiled wax paper and 2 dishtowels. Let the loaves rise in a warm place for 8-12 hours. Bake at 350° for 35-40 minutes in the lower part of the oven to ensure browning on the bottom. Remove from the pans while hot and brush the tops with melted butter. Cool on racks.

Here's an option you may want to try. Instead of using 1½ cups of warm water use 1½ cups of warm potato stock. Just save the stock after you have boiled some potatoes and use it in the bread for a nice variation in flavor.

Karen's Six Week Muffins

I've mentioned elsewhere in this book that Karen Sepich has a way of coming up with some recipes that are real zingers. Good, easy and different. This is one of them and it came along a little too late for us to use it when the children were all at home. I think it would have been great to have this around when the house was full. Try it out, I bet you'll like it too.

1 15-ounce box Raisin Bran
1 cup melted butter
3 cups sugar
4 eggs, beaten
1 quart buttermilk
5 cups flour
5 teaspoons soda
5 teaspoons salt

Prep time: 20 min.
Cook time: 15-20 min./batch
Yield: A bunch

Mix all the dry ingredients in a large mixing bowl. Add the beaten eggs, melted butter and buttermilk to the dry ingredients and mix well. Fill greased muffin tins 2/3 full and bake at 400° for 15-20 minutes. That's all, folks!

Store the unused portion in a sealed container in the refrigerator for up to six weeks! How's that for having a quick breakfast muffin for the hungry munchkins on a school morning?

Here are a few variations that work very well.

• Add 1½ cups of blueberries to enough mix for 12 muffins. Sprinkle with sugar and bake as above.

• Grate or chop 1 large Granny Smith apple into enough mix for 12 muffins. Combine 1 tablespoon of cinnamon with 3 tablespoons of sugar and ¼ cup of chopped pecans and sprinkle on top. Bake as above.

Cover the bottom of the muffin tin with batter. Add small chunks of cream cheese and top with batter. Bake as above.

Banana Nut Bread

This was the first quick bread I really liked. Toasted with butter and served with a cup of good Community coffee, this makes a special moment out of a coffee break. We don't bake it that often and when we do there has always been a question as to which of the 100 or so cookbooks contained the recipe we used last. To mitigate this problem I experimented one day with a combination of several recipes that had variations of the ingredients that I liked. The biggest difference is the use of one cup of whole-wheat flour. Also, many of the recipes call for walnuts but I favor pecans. It's a Southern thing.

8 tablespoons unsalted butter,
   at room temperature
¾ cup sugar
2 eggs
1 cup all-purpose flour
1 cup whole-wheat flour
1 teaspoon baking soda
½ teaspoon salt
3 large ripe bananas, masked
1 teaspoon vanilla
½ cup shelled pecans, coarsely chopped

Prep time: 20 min.
Cook time: 50-50 min.
Yield: 3 small loaves

Preheat the oven to 350°. Using Baker's Joy spray 3 small loaf pans and set aside.

Cream the butter and sugar until it is light and fluffy. Add the eggs one at a time, beating well after each addition. Mix the two flours together and whisk to blend. Mix the flours with the egg, sugar and butter mixture to form a thick batter. Fold in the mashed bananas, vanilla and chopped pecans. Pour the mixture into the prepared loaf pan and bake it for 50-60 minutes, until a cake tester inserted in the middle comes out clean. Cool in the pan for 10 minutes and then cool on a rack.

Slice and serve warm with butter or when the bread is cooled slice and toast it. This bread freezes well and can be made ahead. Makes one loaf, almost 3 pounds or three small loaves.

Arlene's Pumpkin Bread

Arlene Land was the mother of our very good friend, Sara Hoeppner. She lived in Neosho, Missouri. Over the years she and Carol had become close and used to talk on the telephone at length. When Sara and Doug moved back to the Joplin-Neosho area we would always spend some time with Arlene on our trips to visit them. Arlene had, for many years, made countless loaves of this bread at Christmas time and had gifted anybody that she came across with one, or more. Arlene was justifiably proud of the recipe and Carol felt honored when she gave her a copy of it. It's easy and works well paired with Spiced Applesauce Bread and Banana Bread for a brunch.

4 eggs
1 cup Canola oil
3 cups sugar
2 cups cooked, pureed pumpkin (1 can)
3 ½ cups flour
2 teaspoons soda
½ teaspoon salt
2/3 cup water
1 teaspoon cinnamon
1 teaspoon nutmeg
1 teaspoon cloves
1 cup chopped nuts

Prep time: 30 min.
Cook time: 25-30 min.
Yield: 6 small loaves

Preheat the oven to 350°. Beat first four ingredients thoroughly. Add water and flour alternately. Add spices and nuts. Spray 6 small loaf pans with Baker's Joy and pour batter into pan. Bake for 25-30 minutes or until a cake tester inserted in the middle of the loaf comes out clean.

Spiced Applesauce Bread

Some time ago I was asked by the Ladies Club at Blessed Sacrament Church to cook for the Mother/Daughter Communion Breakfast on Sunday morning. We came up with a couple of great recipes for a sausage/egg dish and some fabulous hash browns that are included elsewhere in this book. To go with those two dishes we decided to bake a few loaves of various breads. Arlene's Pumpkin Bread was one of them. This fine applesauce bread was one and we included a really good banana bread, as well. They were all a hit. We found that they all kept very well and could be made ahead of time and frozen. A great idea, when you're trying to avoid the last minute rush.

1 ¼ cups chunky applesauce
1 cup white sugar
½ cup vegetable oil
2 eggs
3 tablespoons milk
2 cups all-purpose flour
1 teaspoon baking soda
½ teaspoon baking powder
½ teaspoon ground cinnamon
¼ teaspoon ground nutmeg
¼ teaspoon ground allspice
¼ teaspoon salt

Prep time: 20 min.
Cook time: 60 min.
Yield: 3 small loaves

Preheat oven to 350°. Using Baker's Joy lightly spray 3 small loaf pans. In a large bowl, combine the applesauce, sugar, oil, eggs and milk; beat well. Sift in the flour, baking soda, baking powder, cinnamon, nutmeg and salt; stir until smooth. At this point you can fold in some chopped pecans, if desired. Pour batter into prepared pans. Bake in a preheated oven for 60 minutes, or until a cake tester inserted into center of the loaf comes out clean.

Turkey Fest at Festival Foods

The Opening Act

The recipes contained in this section present a tough problem. It's hard to know when to quit eating the appetizers and move on to the rest of the meal. Actually, several of these appetizers can be used as a main dish quite easily and time has proven that the Remoulade Sauce is outstanding when served with Fried Catfish. Many of these recipes were used extensively in the catering business with great results. We served a lot of Shrimp Remoulade and it was often used in the conversion of some of the Mid Western palates we encountered.

49	~	Cajun Shrimp Remoulade
50	~	Classic Seafood Cocktail Sauce
51	~	Grilled Shrimp on a Skewer
52	~	Sausage Stuffed Mushrooms
53	~	Beef Roll
54	~	Spinach and Artichoke Dip
55	~	Genuine Buffalo Wings with Frank's Hot Sauce
56	~	Bar Trash
57	~	Black Bean Salsa

Cajun Shrimp Remoulade

I've always been a fan of spicy red sauces or cocktail sauces with seafood. This version of a remoulade sauce made me change my mind. My old friend and workmate, Bob Campbell, and I were getting into some kind of trouble in Lafayette, Louisiana one day and we decided to stop and eat. As mentioned elsewhere in this book, Lafayette has so many good restaurants it's hard to pick a bad one. I don't recall the name of this little place but it was on Johnston Street! I ordered fried frog legs that day and they were served with a Remoulade type of sauce that was incredibly good and according to the proprietor, very easy to fix. I wrote down the recipe, which he readily shared, and then promptly lost it. I've never been back to that restaurant but I've thought of it often because of that sauce. Recently Carol and I were looking for a remoulade recipe and we found several. After some experimentation and minor changes we settled on this one. It is very reminiscent of the taste of that sauce in Lafayette. You could think of this sauce as a "jazzed up" tartar sauce.

1½ cups mayonnaise
½ cup Creole mustard
1 tablespoon Worcestershire sauce
2 teaspoons hot sauce
½ cup finely diced green onions
¼ cup finely diced celery
2 tablespoons finely diced garlic
¼ cup finely chopped parsley
½ tablespoon lemon juice
Salt and fresh ground black pepper to taste

3 pounds boiled shrimp

Prep time 20 min.
Yield: Approx. 2½ cups

In a two-quart mixing bowl, combine the above ingredients, whisking well to blend all of the seasonings. Once blended, cover and place in the refrigerator. It should be chilled for several hours to allow time for the full flavor to develop. This sauce is excellent served with boiled shrimp as an appetizer. We have found it is particularly good with fried catfish and served it many times in the catering business as a premium choice of sauce with the meal. On many occasions when we provided an appetizer tray of fried catfish nuggets we featured this sauce.

Classic Seafood Cocktail Sauce

Belly up to the bar at The Acme Oyster House on Iberville Street in New Orleans and the first thing one of the oyster shuckers will do is to set you up with all of the necessary ingredients to make your own cocktail sauce. Ketchup, Tabasco, lemon juice, horseradish and Worcestershire are all set up in a row. You just put a little of this, a dab of that, a splash of Tabasco and stir it up. If you need a little more of something, just add whatever, until you get it right. That works at the Acme Oyster House, but if you're serving several people a Shrimp Cocktail or Fried Catfish and hush puppies it's a little bit awkward. Never fear, we've taken all of the guesswork out of it in the recipe below. There's no telling how much cocktail sauce we've made but it all started with this recipe. You can double it, triple it and on and on. It always tastes right on. The amount of heat you like is a matter of personal taste and all you have to do is add more Tabasco to get there. This works equally well with boiled shrimp in Shrimp Cocktail and with Fried Catfish.

¾ cup ketchup
1 tablespoon lemon juice
½ teaspoon Worcestershire
½ teaspoon Tabasco
2 teaspoons horseradish

Prep time: 15 min.
Yield: Approx. 1 cup/10 servings

Mix all the ingredients and chill well before serving. This will last several days in the refrigerator. If you're wondering, one gallon of ketchup will make about 215 servings of cocktail sauce!

Grilled Shrimp on a Skewer

Few ingredients are as good as well prepared shrimp. They are good in salads, excellent in appetizers and top drawer as a main dish. We've served this dish as an appetizer and as part of a main dish with grilled steak. Either way they are great. The marinade is the key to the success of this recipe. I like the flavor of fresh cracked black pepper and the fresh garlic is fabulous. Wait until you pull these shrimp from the refrigerator and open up the Ziploc bag. The aroma of fresh garlic and fresh ground black pepper is killer.

2 pounds peeled shrimp (about 30 large shrimp)
1/3 cup canola oil
1/3 cup lemon juice
4 cloves garlic, finely minced
2 teaspoons *Celebration Seasonings All Purpose Seasoning Blend*
½ teaspoon paprika
½ teaspoon cracked black pepper

Prep time: 20 min.
Marinate time: 2 hours
Yield: Approx. 5 appetizer servings

Combine the canola oil, lemon juice, garlic and seasonings. Mix well. Marinate the shrimp in this mixture for about two hours in the refrigerator in a Ziploc bag. Periodically, turn the bag to ensure all the shrimp are evenly coated. When you open the bag be prepared for a garlic blast that will clear your sinuses. Drain and skewer the shrimp with two skewers to keep them from turning. Save the marinade to baste the shrimp when you turn them on the grill. Grill on a hot fire for about 5-6 minutes on a side. I suggest you use more shrimp than you think you need. They go fast.

Sausage Stuffed Mushrooms

This is a favorite appetizer of ours. In the catering business we made these by the hundreds and they were always a hit. This recipe is an evolution of the basic stuffed mushrooms that we used for quite a while.

We wanted some mushrooms with a bit more dash in them and after some experimentation we arrived at this result. The spicy sausage provides a nice complementary taste to the earthy mushroom. We typically use our own breakfast sausage when preparing these mushrooms (recipe found in Breakfast Section) but Jimmy Dean Original breakfast sausage works well. We have also had some good results when using Hot Italian Sausage.

24 large mushrooms
½ pound bulk breakfast sausage
¼ cup diced green onions
1 clove garlic, minced
2 tablespoons fine dry unseasoned bread crumbs
2 tablespoons grated Parmesan cheese
Olive oil

Prep time: 30 min.
Cook time: 30 min.
Yield: Approx. 12 appetizer servings

Clean all of the mushrooms and remove the caps. Trim off and discard the dry end of each stem. Dice the stems and set aside. Brush olive oil on the inside and outside of each mushroom cap and set aside. In a medium saucepan cook the chopped stems, green onions and garlic with the sausage. When this mixture is done, stir in the breadcrumbs first and then the Parmesan cheese. As the cheese melts it will bind the stuffing together and make it easier to stuff the mushrooms. Stuff each mushroom and arrange in a shallow casserole dish or appropriate sized tray. Bake at 325° for 25 minutes. Serve hot.

These can be prepared well ahead of time and held in the refrigerator until time to cook.

Beef Roll

Here's a great example of an old time family recipe. Nobody seems to know where it came from or when; it's just been around in Carol's family for a long time. Over the years Carol had made this from time to time and we always loved it. It's a bit of a hassle to make, which is probably why she didn't make it more often. When Brandon and I were researching the menu for Celebration Catering, this recipe just popped out as a great appetizer. We offered it as a Beef Summer Sausage tray and served it with Zatarain's Creole Mustard. We rarely had any left over and we made some very large batches of it. The recipe calls for five pounds of lean ground meat. It can be cut down but we always reasoned that if you are going to go through all the steps to make this you might as well make at least a full five pounds. It worked for us!

5 pounds of lean ground beef (the leaner the better)
¼ cup meat cure salt (available at most stores)
2½ tablespoons black pepper (I prefer fresh ground)
1 tablespoon red pepper (cayenne)
1 tablespoon mustard seed
1½ teaspoons garlic powder
2½ tablespoons liquid smoke (Hickory or Mesquite)

Prep time: 20 min./ day for 3 days
Cook time: 6-8 hrs
Yield: 5-1 lb logs

Mix all of the seasonings well. Place the ground beef in a large bowl and pour the seasoning all over the mixture. Knead the beef until the seasoning is incorporated throughout. Cover the bowl and place it in the refrigerator. For the next two days take the mixture out and knead it well. It will be stiff and the coloration will get darker each day. On the third day take the mixture out and separate it into 5 portions. Roll each portion into a log being careful to get out as many air pockets as possible. Place the logs on a rack in a preheated 200° oven for 6 hours. Make sure the logs don't touch. At three hours turn them. They will be a dark, rich red and the smell is absolutely great. At six hours take the beef sticks out and pat the excess oil off of them. They can now be sliced and served or cooled, wrapped and refrigerated. They will keep well in the refrigerator for several days. They can be frozen as well. I can't tell you how long because they never lasted more than a day or so in our house. For a different texture these beef rolls can be cooked for 8 hours at 175°. You will get the same taste but a softer texture.

Spinach and Artichoke Dip

This recipe showed up in several cookbooks with some different proportions. After some trial and error blending elements we liked in several recipes this was the final result. Some recipes called for using cooked spinach but we felt it wasn't necessary since spinach is so tender and cooks so readily. Whether or not it was cooked didn't seem to make a difference in the taste. Carol makes some great toast points with a thin sliced Pepperidge Farm bread that work very well with this dip. It can be put together beforehand and held in the refrigerator if needed and heated prior to serving.

¼ pound unsalted butter
1 medium onion chopped
4 large cloves garlic, minced
4 tablespoons flour
1 tablespoon Dijon mustard
1 tablespoon *Celebration Seasonings Cajun Style All Purpose Seasoning Blend*
2 cups milk, heated
½ cup grated Pecorino Romano
½ cup grated Gruyere
1 cup heavy cream
1 10-ounce bag fresh baby spinach, chopped
3 6-ounce jars marinated artichokes, drained and chopped

Prep time: 20 min.
Cook time: 30 min.
Yield: Approx. 4 ½ cups

Melt the butter in a large heavy bottomed saucepan and sauté the onions and garlic until tender. Stir in the flour and blend well to make a white roux. Do not brown the roux. Add the Dijon mustard and the *Celebration Seasonings Cajun Style All Purpose Seasoning Blend* and stir in well. Remove from the heat and add the milk that has been heated in another pan. Whisk this mixture well and return to the heat to simmer. Add the cheeses and simmer until the cheeses melt. Add the cream, chopped spinach and artichokes. Heat the mixture until hot. Serve with toast points.

Genuine Buffalo Wings With Frank's Red Hot Sauce

This recipe is an example of blatant theft. When we were in the catering business we had several requests for Hot Wings. One day, Brandon walked into the banquet hall and said he had tried this recipe and it was great. We cooked up a batch and it was obvious that he had understated the results. They were immediately placed on the catering menu and we served them many times with much success. The recipe is printed right on the side of the bottle of Frank's Original Red Hot Cayenne Pepper Sauce! When you read the proportions in the recipe you might have the first impression that it will be blazing hot. Not so! These wings are well seasoned with a nice crisp texture. Serve them with impunity; your guests will love them. There are a couple of key steps in the recipe that make these wings great. First, they are fried for 12 minutes, which makes the wings very crispy. Secondly, and very importantly, the butter is clarified. If the butter is not clarified it will not mix well with the hot sauce. Cut this corner and you will be sorry. Also, it is not necessary to season the wings before frying them.

¾ cup Frank's Original Red Hot
   Cayenne Pepper Sauce
½ cup hot clarified butter
5 pounds thawed chicken wings
   (roughly 1 dozen/pound)

Prep time: 30 min.
Cook time: 12 min.
Yield: Approx. 6 dozen

Combine Frank's Original Red Hot and clarified butter in a large bowl; mix well. Deep-fry the chicken wings at 350º for 12 minutes until crispy brown; drain well. Add to sauce and toss well to coat the wings. Serve with bleu cheese dip and celery sticks. This recipe expands easily...just be sure to keep the proportions the same. We've fried as many as 60 pounds for an event!

Bar Trash

Any appetizer with a name like this is worth trying. We were in New Orleans and saw this on a menu. It is quite simple to make and tastes great. In my opinion it could do well as an entrée. This would be an opportunity to try out the *Creole Butter* found in the *Lagniappe* section of this book.

¼ pound small peeled raw shrimp
¼ pound crawfish
¼ pound firm white fish cut into chunks
¼ pound scallops (preferably bay scallops, if you can find them)
4 finely diced green onions
Butter
Celebration Seasonings Cajun Style All-Purpose Seasoning Blend to taste

Prep time: 20 min.
Cook time: 15 min.
Yield: 4-6 servings

Prepare the seafood and the green onions and set aside. Heat the butter in the skillet, add the seafood and sauté lightly. Season to taste when seafood is almost done and garnish with the green onions. Serve with garlic bread.

Black Bean Salsa

Each summer for three years running, I catered an all day affair during which we served three meals for 125 people. Even though our menu was quite different from the other caterers here in LaCrosse, Wisconsin, I sometimes forgot that, and in an effort to keep things new and fresh, I kept adding different dishes. Once, while talking to the person responsible for arranging this event I got carried away and suggested that we serve a nice fresh Black Bean Salsa with the luncheon. She thought that was a wonderful suggestion and told me to go ahead and do it. Now wasn't that nice! I had never made Black Bean Salsa before, ever. Below is the result. It was so good it immediately became a regularly listed item on our menu and we served it many times. This recipe expands easily. For parties around the house, I normally make triple the amount shown here. Interestingly, we have found that this dish works equally as well as a side dish and an appetizer.

¼ cup canola oil
3 tablespoons fresh lime juice
2 teaspoons ground cumin
1 teaspoon red wine vinegar
1 can (15 ounces) black beans
½ cup finely diced yellow bell pepper
½ cup finely diced red onion
½ cup finely diced Roma tomatoes
¼ cup chopped green onions
2 teaspoons minced garlic
1 tablespoon finely diced fresh basil

Prep time: 30 min.
Yields: 4 servings

Mix the canola oil, lime juice, cumin and red wine vinegar together and set aside. Drain and rinse beans and set aside. Finely dice the remaining ingredients and mix them with the beans. Pour the oil and vinegar mixture over the diced vegetables and mix well. Chill before serving. This can be made a day ahead and held in the refrigerator.

More wine for the hostess

The Warm Up

You might be a Cajun if you say 70° F is a "cool snap" and it's gumbo weather! With that measuring stick you can bet nobody has to wait very long for "gumbo weather" in Wisconsin! That has proven to be one aspect of living in the Mid-West I have found most enjoyable. As a matter of fact, it has given me sufficient incentive to search out some really terrific cold weather soups and stews. This section contains some great old classic Cajun recipes, but there are some soul warming additions that just beg for a cold Saturday afternoon to be enjoyed.

Like all of the recipes in this book these soups have had plenty of use and are proven hits. Carol and I have found that these soups served in small portions are great additions to a several course menu, but all work quite well as a stand-alone hearty soup.

61 ~ **Louisiana Style Oyster Stew**

62 ~ **Roux**

63 ~ **Chicken And Sausage Gumbo**

64 ~ **Double Cheese French Onion Soup**

65 ~ **Steak Pottage**

66 ~ **Seafood Court Bouillon**

68 ~ **Real Chili**

70 ~ **Triple Flavored Wild Rice Soup**

71 ~ **Turkey Bone Soup**

Louisiana Style Oyster Stew

Henry Arceneaux was my boss when we lived in New Orleans. It was customary for all of us in his department to work late. On many occasions we would meet for a couple of beers at Jimmy Liuzza's neighborhood bar and then take in a late night meal in one of the million or so restaurants in New Orleans. Henry knew restaurants in the city as well as he knew how to cook good food. A meal in New Orleans with Henry would typically encompass three or four restaurants. It was like dining with a food critic.

Annually our department would have a four or five day retreat at Fountainbleu State Park, located north of Lake Ponchatrain near Mandeville, Louisiana. Henry did most of the cooking and this was one of our favorite appetizers. I have searched for a long time and have never found a recipe for oyster stew written like this. Every one I have ever seen has required the use of milk or half and half. This one uses the oyster water as the liquid. I think that is the reason it can be seasoned so well.

1 quart oysters
1 bell pepper, minced
2 stalk celery, minced
4 green onions, minced
1 stick butter
Flour
Celebration Seasonings Cajun Style All Purpose Seasoning Blend, to taste

Prep time: 30 min.
Cook time: 45 min.
Yield: Approx. 4 quarts

Drain oysters and save the liquid. Mince the bell pepper, celery, and green onions and set aside. Make a light roux using the butter and flour. When the roux just begins to darken add the minced bell pepper and celery. Cook over low heat until the celery wilts. Thin the roux with the liquid drained from the oysters. If more liquid is needed to attain the right consistency, simply add water to the oysters and drain again. The secret is to use the oyster-flavored water as stock. When the roux is the right consistency, season with *Celebration Seasonings Cajun Style All Purpose Seasoning Blend,* to taste. Add oysters 3-5 minutes before serving. Just before serving add the minced green onions. This makes great appetizer soup.

Roux

Roux, essentially browned flour and oil, is the basis for a large number of Cajun dishes. It acts as a thickener in such classic recipes as gumbo, sauce piquant, seafood court bouillon and of course many others. Additionally, it brings a full-bodied flavor to the pot that cannot be achieved by any other means I know. Many recipes call for various shades of roux: blond, medium or dark. A good Cajun rule of thumb for the shade of roux you need is simply this: light meat, dark roux and dark meat, light roux. It is noteworthy that virtually all recipes I have ever read for gumbo call for a dark roux. There are exceptions but this is a good guide.

I recommend using a large flat-bottomed cast iron pot to make a roux, because of its even heat transfer properties. A roux can certainly be made in any heavy-bottomed pot, but you need to be aware of how your particular pot transfers heat. Another preference of mine is to use a wooden spatula to stir the roux with as it cooks. Also be very careful not to splash any of the hot roux on you when you're stirring it. They don't call it "Cajun napalm" without good reason.

There is considerable debate about the portions of flour and oil necessary for a roux. As I mentioned in the gumbo recipe there are as many versions as there are people that cook it and everybody does it the right way. I hold no method as right or wrong, but I'll tell you what works for me. A basic roux consists of slightly more flour than oil. I use 1½ cups of oil to 2 cups of flour. I suggest cooking it on low to medium heat until you become accustomed to the process. It is easy to burn a roux, which you cannot use, unless you like a burnt taste in your final dish! Start slow at first, heating the oil and stirring in the flour. Continue to stir until the mixture darkens to the color you desire. Once you master this technique you can turn the heat up and make the roux faster. My preferred method is to start by heating the oil to about 300°. I then pour the flour in gradually while stirring continuously to blend the mixture. Stir constantly and adjust the heat downward as the flour begins to darken. It takes practice to develop a feel for the process. A nice medium roux is about the color of a Kraft caramel candy. If you stop before that you will have a blond roux...if you proceed beyond that you will have a dark roux. You be the judge. Just remember...it takes patience and practice.

CHICKEN STOCK

3 lbs. chicken bones
1 onion, coarsely chopped
2 celery stalks, cut in 3-inch lengths

Simmer the chicken stock several hours before you start to cook the gumbo. I buy chicken breasts with the rib cage intact and then de-bone them for use in the gumbo. The rib cage is then used in the stock. Do not use any salt in the stock. Strain the stock before starting the gumbo.
Make a roux first and set it aside on the stovetop to keep it warm.

Chicken And Sausage Gumbo

Gumbo is quite likely one of the most recognizable of Cajun dishes, and there are probably as many recipes and methods for cooking it as there are people who cook it. That can be both good and bad. Good because it's hard to botch it up, bad because everybody in South Louisiana is an authority on the subject. Naturally, after more than 40 years of cooking gumbo, I have developed my own methods, which like all the other recipes contain many of the same elements.

In all of my recipes, I use basic stock for the liquid. I have included a recipe for chicken stock below. I don't like to use a commercially available product because of the high salt content that, among other things, has an impact on the seasoning process.

After some experimentation you may very well decide to do something differently in the recipe and that's great. Keep notes. Here is a good basic gumbo recipe to use for a starting point.

2 lbs. cubed chicken breast
1 lb. smoked sausage (sliced in
   1/8 inch rounds)
1 medium onion, diced
1 bell pepper, diced
3 celery stalks, diced
4 cloves garlic, crushed
6 quarts chicken stock (recipe above)
2 cups flour
2 cups canola oil
1 tsp. Liquid Smoke
*Celebration Seasonings Cajun Style All-
   Purpose Seasoning Blend*, to taste

Prep time: Approx. 1 hour
Cook time: 2 hours
Yield: 7 quarts

With your stock set aside and the roux made, you are now ready to make a gumbo. First, brown the sausage for about ten minutes. When the sausage is starting to stick to the pot add the chicken and brown for another ten minutes or until the mixture starts to stick to the pot again. Add the diced seasoning vegetables and cook until the onion is wilted. The onion, bell pepper and celery will release juices that will begin to deglaze the pot. Be sure to scrape the bottom and sides of the pot to break loose all of the bits and pieces of chicken and sausage that might have stuck to it. When this is done, add 4 quarts of the chicken stock to the pot. Bring this mixture to a hard simmer and add a teaspoon of liquid smoke. The mixture should now be somewhat dark in color. Season to taste with Celebration Seasonings Cajun Style All-Purpose Seasoning Blend and allow it to simmer for about 30 minutes. Add 1 to 1 ½ cups of the roux to the stock mixture and let it dissolve. The gumbo should now be a dark caramel color. Continue to simmer until the chicken is done and tender. Add additional roux or stock to achieve the thickness you like. Check for seasoning often during the process and adjust as needed. Serve over hot cooked rice.

Double Cheese French Onion Soup

One of Carol's favorite soups is a good French onion soup. We've tried it at many restaurants with a real mixed bag of results. Some have too much onion or too much cheese. We've had bad croutons and a lousy base as well. After enough misfires Carol decided it was time to get in the kitchen and come up with a consistently good soup for our own use. Here it is. Like most of the recipes in this book it's fairly straightforward and easy.

4 large onions
½ cup butter
1 tablespoon flour
1 10 ½ ounce can of undiluted
   chicken broth
1 10 ½ ounce can of undiluted beef broth
2 cups water
¼ cup white wine
¼ teaspoon black pepper (fresh ground)
8 ¾-inch slices French bread, toasted
8 slices mozzarella cheese
½ cup grated Parmigiano Reggiano cheese

Prep time: 30 min.
Cook time: About 45 min.
Yield: 8 cups

Sauté onions in butter in a Dutch oven until tender. Blend in the flour and stir until smooth. Gradually add the chicken broth, beef broth, water and white wine. Bring to a boil, reduce the heat and simmer 15 minutes. Add the pepper.

Place eight ovenproof serving bowls on a baking sheet. Place 1 toasted bread slice in each bowl and ladle the soup over the bread. Top with one slice of mozzarella cheese and sprinkle with grated Parmigiano Reggiano. Place the baking sheet under the broiler about 6 inches from heat until the cheese melts and starts to toast.

Steak Pottage

In my last work assignment before retiring I worked in Appleton, Wisconsin. While there I made the acquaintance of an outstanding gentleman, the late Gary Christopherson. We shared a lot of common background in the industry, not to mention we were the same age and were both on the last train out of the corporate world. Gary and I used to break away on occasion and go out to a game farm and shoot traps. It was a great way to blow off a little steam, if you will pardon the pun. Whatever we "killed" we didn't have to worry about dressing and cooking. It wasn't even necessary to pick up the pieces of the clay pigeons. We would just shoot a few rounds and talk about "stuff." We didn't talk about work very much, but we certainly covered a wide range of other topics! One of Gary's favorite subjects was Alaska, where he and his wife, Ruby, had lived and worked for many years. I always encouraged those stories, because I have never been there and know little of Alaska. He told some interesting tales, to be sure. One day when we were talking about cold weather, a subject common to both Alaska and Wisconsin, we veered off on the subject of the wonderful warming properties of a good soup. That's a logical transition, isn't it? Gary talked about this pottage like it was an old friend. He later gave me this recipe and I, too, have enjoyed it ever since. It has the basic attributes I always look for in a soup: simple, robust and warm. What else is there to look for in a soup?

1 cup diced onions
¾ cup diced celery
1 cup diced carrots
1 cup butter
¾ cup all purpose flour
1 pound lean ground sirloin
8 cups cold water
1¼ cups diced tomatoes in puree
2 teaspoons black pepper
1 teaspoon minced garlic
2 ounces beef base dissolved in water
1 10-ounce package frozen mixed vegetables

Prep time: 30 min.
Cook time: 1½ hour
Yield: 12 servings

Preheat the oven to 350º. Press the ground sirloin onto a baking sheet not more that one inch thick. Bake it until well browned. Drain well and break into chunks about 1 inch in size and set aside.

Cook the onions, celery and carrots in butter over medium heat until the onions are transparent. Add flour and whisk until smooth. Cook until the mixture begins to bubble around the edges. Watch the heat on this step and be careful not to overcook. The mixture is thick and has a tendency to stick. Add half the water to the cooked vegetable mixture and cook until the mixture begins to boil lightly. Add the tomatoes, ground beef, pepper, garlic and beef base. Stir well to incorporate all of the ingredients but do not break up the beef chunks. Cook for about 10 minutes uncovered. The soup will be very thick at this stage. Add the remaining water and frozen vegetables and simmer until the vegetables are done. Do not allow soup to boil. Serve hot. This soup refrigerates well and is excellent heated up the next day. This recipe makes about 12 servings and expands easily.

Seafood Court Bouillon

This is, quite likely, my most favorite seafood dish. The translation of Court Bouillon literally means "short soup." There are so many variations on this basic recipe that a whole chapter could be devoted to it! I have eaten it in many of its variants and, in truth, would be hard pressed to choose a favorite. There is, however, one that stands out. Not long ago, our old friends Billy Ray and Beverly Stokes came to visit Carol and me in LaCrosse, Wisconsin. While they were here we invited several close friends over for the evening. I happened to have about three pounds of crabmeat in the freezer that I had been hoarding for a special occasion. Additionally, I happened to have several pounds of catfish filets and several pounds of shrimp. This was not going to be an ordinary rendition of this dish! Nor was it going to be an ordinary evening. For Carol and me to share an evening with some of our oldest and dearest friends in addition to a group of our closest friends in LaCrosse was a true delight. I should probably say that this is a fairly lengthy recipe that takes some time to cook. My feelings are that if you are going to commit the time necessary to prepare this dish, you might as well make it worth your while and make a lot of it! Here's the recipe.

14 Good friends marinated in various shades red and white wine and set aside
5 pounds catfish filets
5 pounds shrimp, peeled and de-veined (save the shells)
3 pounds lump crabmeat (since that's what I had)
2 medium onions, diced
2 stalks celery, diced
1 bell pepper, diced
2 cloves garlic, diced
1 bunch green onions, diced and set aside
1 ¾ cups oil, in all
2 gallons water
2-28 oz. cans crushed tomatoes in puree
1 can Rotel tomatoes
Cooked white rice
Celebration Seasonings Cajun Style All Purpose Seasoning Blend, to taste

Prep time: 1 hour
Cook time: About 2 hours
Yield: Approx. 8 quarts

Cut the catfish into bite-sized pieces and set aside. Peel and de-vein the shrimp and set aside. Make a stock using the shrimp shells, three stalks of celery and one quartered onion. Simmer these ingredients in 2 gallons of water for two to three hours while you are preparing everything else. The longer you can simmer the stock, the better. Do not use any other seasoning in this stock. If, after you have completed the recipe, you have excess stock, freeze it for use another time.

Dice the onions, celery, bell pepper and garlic and mix them together. Dice the green onions and set them aside. They are the last ingredient you will use in this recipe.

Now you make a roux using 1½ cups of cooking oil and two cups of flour. See the Roux recipe in this section. Once the roux is made set it aside on the stovetop and keep it warm.

Heat ¼ cup of cooking oil in a large soup kettle. Add the diced vegetables and cook until the onions are wilted. Add the crushed tomatoes and the Rotel tomatoes and cook uncovered for about 45 minutes or until the oil and tomatoes separate. Now add 1 gallon of the shrimp stock and simmer for 30 minutes. In the next step you should add about one cup of the roux to the stock and stir well. Simmer for 30 minutes. At this stage of preparation the stock should be a dark reddish-brown color. Now is a good time to season the Court Bouillon for the first time. After allowing the seasoning to permeate the stock and the roux to thoroughly dissolve, use the remaining stock and/or the remaining roux to adjust the thickness of the broth as necessary. Cook about 15 minutes to allow everything to stabilize.

Add the crabmeat and simmer for about 15 minutes, after which I would suggest testing your seasoning. Now add the catfish and shrimp and cook for 15 minutes. Test once again for seasoning. My preference is for the dish to have a little heat but that is an individual taste. A few minutes before serving sprinkle the green onions over the top of the Court Bouillon. Not only does this add a burst of flavor but the color combination makes a nice presentation. Serve this over cooked white rice with green salad and toasted garlic bread.

Real Chili

During one of the three times we lived in Baton Rouge, Louisiana, my friend Doug Hoeppner found this recipe for chili. As I recall, it had been published in the Baton Rouge Morning Advocate as a prize-winning chili recipe from the Great Texas Chili Cook Off in Austin, Texas. I ate the chili at Doug and Sara's house one time and thought it was great. I found out later that Doug had entered a chili cook off in Baton Rouge with this recipe and had won! I didn't cook the recipe for several years because it makes a large amount and we never had that many people coming over to eat who wanted chili.

In about 1992 one of the local banks in LaCrosse, Wisconsin, where we now live, sponsored a chili cook off to benefit the DARE drug awareness program. I thought it would be fun to enter this recipe, so I got a friend of mine to enter with me. Since Frank Roldan is Cuban, we thought it might lend a little dignity to the affair. Well, at least he speaks Spanish! Would you believe, the judges didn't even give us an also-ran! I'm not bitter about this, but the judges were the Festmaster and his entourage from the LaCrosse Octoberfest. Maybe if we had cooked some bratwurst in that chili we might have garnered some recognition!

Fast forward to 2005 and I am pleased to add a postscript to this storied recipe. I have the good fortune to be associated with a group of gentlemen in the LaCrosse area known as The Gentlemen Gourmands. In October 2005, in the DARE Chili Cook Off, the Gourmands entered

2 tablespoons paprika
1 tablespoon oregano
11 tablespoons chili powder
4 tablespoons cumin
4 tablespoons beef bouillon
   (instant crushed)
3 cans beer
2 cups water
2 pounds pork, cubed
2 pounds beef chuck, cubed
6 pounds ground rump
4 large onions, finely chopped
10 cloves garlic, finely chopped
Vegetable oil as needed
1 teaspoon mole (also called
   mole poblano)
1 tablespoon sugar
2 tablespoons coriander seeds
1 teaspoon hot sauce
1 8-ounce can tomato puree
2 14.5-ounce cans of Rotel tomatoes
1 tablespoon Masa Harina flour
Salt to taste

Prep time: 1 hour
Cook time: 2 hours
Yield: Approx. 1 gal.

In a large cast iron pot, add paprika, oregano, chili powder, cumin, beef bouillon, beer and 2 cups of water. Let simmer. In a separate cast iron skillet brown 2 pounds meat with 1 tablespoon of oil. Drain and add to simmering spices. Continue until all meat is browned. I cook this outside on a propane cooker with four burners. If you use two skillets this step goes a lot faster.

Sauté finely chopped onions and garlic in 1 tablespoon of oil. Add to spices and meat mixture. Add water as needed. Simmer

this recipe and won first place in the non-professional division. Unfortunately, I was out of town but had provided them with the appropriate utensils and the recipe. Since the judging is now by a popular vote cast by all the visitors to the cook off, it should be duly noted that John Wettstein is a consummate salesman. I am told he provided a clinic in how to work a crowd. Congratulations to the Gourmands. I feel vindicated, if only vicariously!

And now... yet another postscript. In the DARE Chili Cook Off in October 2006, the Gentlemen Gourmands again won their division with this great chili and I was present for the affair. Ahhhh! The sweet taste of success...even if we were in a division that couldn't have had more than three or four entries. In truth, even though the rules required entrants to make about 10 gallons of chili, we made approximately 35 gallons and gave it all away to testers...1/2 ladle at a time!

Here's the recipe. It may seem a little daunting at first but it's really not hard to cook. It just takes a little time. We've found that a few cold beers work wonders in making the time pass.

two hours. Add mole, sugar, coriander, hot sauce, tomato puree and Rotel tomatoes. Simmer 45 minutes. Dissolve Masa Harina flour in warm water and add to chili. Add salt to taste. Simmer 30 minutes. For hotter chili, add more hot sauce.

Triple Flavored Wild Rice Soup

Karen and Chris Sepich are good friends of ours who we see quite often. We are the godparents of their two lovely daughters. Karen always seems to have these really neat recipes that just kind of happen. I don't know where they come from but every once in a while I snatch one and save it. This is one of the saves. I love pretty much anything cooked with rice...it's part of my heritage. I've been told that wild rice is not really rice, but it's close enough for me. We have found that it is difficult to serve this soup as an appetizer because nobody wants to stop eating it! Something this good shouldn't be this easy to prepare. We use the best smoked bacon we can find (currently that's Wright's Hickory Smoked Bacon from Sam's). The smell of onions sautéed in the same skillet this bacon is cooked in is exquisite.

½ cup uncooked wild rice
1½ cups water
½ pound good bacon
¼ cup chopped onion
2½ cups grated American cheese
1 quart half and half (milk if preferred)
2 cans of cream of potato soup
1 can of liquid (½ milk, ½ water)

Prep time: 30 min.
Cook time: Approx 30 min.
Yield: 2½ quarts

Cook wild rice for about 45 minutes in 1½ cups of water. Drain and set aside. In a large pot, fry the bacon and set aside to drain. Pour off most of the bacon grease from the pot. Add the onions to the pot and sauté them until they are wilted. Add the remaining ingredients and the bacon to the onions and cook over medium heat until the grated cheese is melted. Stir often to prevent sticking. Served hot this makes an excellent appetizer soup and it's not too shabby as a stand-alone meal on a cold winter night.

Turkey Bone Soup

I long ago lost count of the number of turkeys I've fried. After having tossed enough turkey carcasses to make an ocean of stock, I decided to save a couple and make a soup. It was well worth the effort. This is a fine soup recipe that uses all of the leftover turkey you have after Thanksgiving or Christmas as well as the whole turkey carcass. Start off with a rich turkey stock made using the carcass that has simmered for several hours. With that for a basis it is hard to go wrong. The recipe also calls for the addition of a light roux at the end of the process to thicken the soup. The roux adds another dimension to the taste of the mixture. I might add that dumplings introduced as a last ingredient make this soup a classic cold weather elixir.

For the Stock

1 whole turkey carcass
1 large onion, roughly chopped
5 stalks celery
Water to cover the carcass, about two gallons

Simmer several hours until the carcass falls apart. Strain the stock and set aside for use in the soup. Pick any left over meat from the carcass and save for the soup. Save and freeze any extra stock for another soup when you don't have the turkey bones handy.

For the Soup

1 large onion, diced
4 stalks celery, diced
1 pound small carrots
8 small to medium Yukon Gold potatoes,
    washed and cubed
1 pound frozen green peas
Leftover turkey, at least 1 ½ -2 pounds, diced
Turkey stock, about 1 gallon
Light roux (1/4 pound butter, 2/3 cup of flour)
    cooked to a light golden brown
*Celebration Seasoning Cajun Style All Purpose
    Seasoning Blend,* to taste

Prep time: 30 min.
Cook time: 1½ hour
Yield: Approx. 5 quarts

Sauté diced onion and celery in a small amount of butter until the onions are wilted. Add stock and simmer for 30 minutes until the celery is tender. Add the potatoes and carrots, and cook until they can be pierced easily with a fork. Add the frozen peas and turkey and cook until the peas are thawed and warm. Add enough roux to achieve the thickness you like. If you wish to add dumplings (I would suggest using the dough from Tim's Never Fail Lighter Than Air Buttermilk Biscuits) do so now and cook, covered, until they are done, about 15 minutes. What a great wintertime meal.

Celebrating our anniversary with a hundred, or so, friends and family

Green Is Good

When I was growing up, salad consisted of iceberg lettuce and French dressing. I didn't like French dressing so I ate my iceberg lettuce with salt and pepper. Not particularly interesting, as salads go. Over the years Carol and I began to broaden our horizons a little and would order a salad when we went out to eat. It has only been in recent years that we have developed a heightened interest in salads and begun to experiment with various greens, dressings, cheeses, nuts and fruits in different combinations. The results have been both gratifying and very good. We have found that the various textures and tastes introduced into a salad bring a refreshing quality to the salad and create some interest in a course that often is dull. To be honest, some of our friends have dubbed Carol "The Salad Maven," a well-earned moniker, to be sure.

Included in this section you will find some very interesting combinations of ingredients. We prefer to grate our own cheese and use a lot of Pecorino Romano, Parmigiano Reggiano, Gorgonzola and Bleu Cheese. Toasted pecans, walnuts, almond slivers and pine nuts add a special crunch in a fresh salad. Whenever possible we use arugula, mache, watercress (when we can find it) Romaine, spinach, Bibb and sometimes even a little iceberg. We often use the prepackaged Spring Mix which contains a little of everything. Fruits we commonly use include strawberries, pears, Mandarin oranges, some wonderful poached pears and most recently fresh peaches.

Dressings are a work of art in themselves and we use several. We seldom use a store bought dressing. It's too much fun to make your own. One lone example of a good commercially obtainable dressing that we like is Brianna's Blush Wine Vinaigrette, which works wonderfully with strawberries and spinach.

Let's go make some salad.

74 ~ **Fruit Salad with Blackberry-Basil Vinaigrette**

75 ~ **Spinach Salad with Blueberry Vinaigrette**

76 ~ **Baby Spinach Salad with Strawberries, Red Onion and Strawberry Vinaigrette**

77 ~ **Sensation Salad**

78 ~ **Classic Green Salad I and II**

79 ~ **Marion's Salad Dressing**

80 ~ **Poached Pears in Red Wine**

81 ~ **Ceasar Salad**

82 ~ **Classic Potato Salad**

83 ~ **Cole Slaw**

84 ~ **Fruit Salad**

Fruit Salad with Blackberry-Basil Vinaigrette

Brandon's wife, Abby, turned up this spectacular salad recipe. As I'm told the inspiration came from a couple of different cooking magazines that were featuring fresh salads. This salad highlights some tastes and textures that just aren't seen in combination everyday and it is guaranteed to garner some rave reviews.

8 cups gourmet salad greens
1 ½ cups sliced mango
1 ½ cups sliced fresh strawberries
1 cup blackberries
1 large avocado sliced

Toss all ingredients in a large bowl and serve immediately with Blackberry-Basil Vinaigrette. Arrange the salads on the plate to assure each serving has some of each of the ingredients.

Blackberry-Basil Vinaigrette

½ (10 ounce) jar seedless
    blackberry preserves
¼ cup red wine vinegar
6 fresh basil leaves
1 garlic clove, sliced
½ teaspoon salt
½ teaspoon seasoned pepper
¾ cup vegetable oil

Prep time: 20 min.
Yield: 8 generous salads

Pulse blackberry preserves, red wine vinegar, and the next 4 ingredients in a blender 2 or 3 times until blended. With the blender running, pour vegetable oil through the food chute in a steady stream: Process until smooth. Chill before serving.

Spinach Salad with Blueberry Vinaigrette

This salad is similar to the Fruit Salad with Blackberry-Basil Vinaigrette. The use of sweet fruits with tart vinegar, along with variations in texture, makes a very appealing presentation for a summer salad. Once we got on this salad train the combinations just seem to keep popping up everywhere.

2 bunches leaf spinach, washed and trimmed
1 pint fresh blueberries
2/3 cup crumbled bleu cheese
½ cup roasted pecans
Red onion rings for garnish

Rinse spinach and pat dry. In a bowl, combine the spinach, the blueberries, cheese and toasted pecans. Add dressing and toss to mix well. Garnish with red onion rings.

Blueberry Vinaigrette

1 shallot
½ pint fresh blueberries
3 tablespoons sugar
1 teaspoon salt
1/3 cup raspberry vinegar
1 cup vegetable oil

Prep time: 20 min.
Yield: 8 generous salads

Combine all ingredients in a blender or food processor and blend until smooth. Chill before serving.

Baby Spinach Salad With Strawberries, Red Onion And Strawberry Vinaigrette

In our quest for salads that look good and taste good this one came early and it will be here late. It's all about the freshness of the ingredients and the presentation. When entertaining it's always nice to have some special salad plates hanging around to enhance the presentation. Good friends Dan and Judy Thelen gave us a gift a while back of some outstanding salad plates made in the shape of a large leaf. They make any salad look great. We have used Brianna's Blush Vinaigrette with this salad, but the included recipe for Strawberry Vinaigrette is superb. Here's the salad.

12 ounces fresh washed baby spinach
1 dozen large fresh sliced strawberries
4 slices a fresh red onion
Strawberry Vinaigrette
Fresh ground black pepper

Prep time: 20 min
Yield: 8 generous salads

Arrange the greens and the strawberries on the salad plate. Separate the sliced onion into rings and arrange several rings on each plate. Dress with Strawberry Vinaigrette and top with fresh ground black pepper.

Strawberry Vinaigrette

¼ cup sugar
1 teaspoon salt
2-3 strawberries
1/3 cup white wine vinegar (red wine vinegar works well also)
1 cup vegetable oil
1 tablespoon poppy seeds

Prep time: 15 min.
Yield: About 8 servings

Mix well in a blender and stir in 1 tablespoon of poppy seeds. Chill and serve over salad.

According to the introduction in the cookbook from the Oxbow Restaurant now located in St. Francisville, Louisiana, this salad dressing was made famous by the old Bob and Jake's Restaurant that was located on Government Street in Baton Rouge. The restaurant, which closed many years ago, was for a long time considered the class of Baton Rouge restaurants. We found the recipe from Bob and Jake's in another cookbook and compared it to the one from The Oxbow. They are both good but this is the one we favor. As with all of our salads we have found that freshly grated Pecorino Romano cheese improves the taste considerably.

½ cup olive oil
½ cup salad oil
1½ tablespoon fresh minced garlic
3 tablespoons fresh lemon juice
1½ teaspoon oregano leaves, not ground
½ teaspoon salt
¾ teaspoon fresh ground black pepper
½ cup grated Pecorino Romano cheese
2 tablespoons flat Italian parsley, chopped

Prep time: 15 min.
Yield: Approx. 1 cup

Put all the above ingredients in a blender and puree for 1 minute. Store in a tightly sealed 1-pint container and chill. When ready to serve, shake well and toss with romaine lettuce and serve immediately. This dressing holds well in the refrigerator for several days but it rarely lasts that long without being eaten.

Classic Green Salad

Here are two green salads that Carol first experimented with quite some time ago. We have used them for several years and they never fail to provide a great salad course for any type of dinner party. They can be served as simply as you wish or with a little presentation can be made as elegant as the situation requires.

Classic Green Salad I

8 cups fresh, washed and drained spring mix
2/3 cup crumbled Gorgonzola cheese
½ cup toasted pecans
Poached Pears (see recipe)
Marion's Salad Dressing (see recipe)

Prep time: 20 min.
Yield: 8 generous salads

Wash and pat dry the fresh spring mix. Prepare the pears and the salad dressing ahead of time according to the recipe. To assemble the salad place the greens in a large bowl and add the toasted pecans, poached pears and Gorgonzola cheese. Add the dressing and toss lightly. Serve immediately. For a more elegant presentation Carol will plate the salad and add the ingredients on each plate.

Classic Green Salad II

8 cups fresh, washed and drained spring mix
2/3 cup shredded Parmigiano Reggiano
½ cup toasted almond slivers
1 small can Mandarin orange slices
Red onion rings for garnish
Marion's Salad Dressing (see recipe)

Prep time: 20 min.
Yield: 8 generous salads

Wash and pat dry the fresh spring mix. Prepare salad dressing ahead of time according to the recipe. To assemble the salad place the greens in a large bowl and add the toasted almonds, Mandarin orange slices and Parmesana Reggiano cheese. Add the dressing and toss lightly. Serve immediately. As with the above salad Carol will plate it individually for a classier presentation.

Marion's Salad Dressing

Buz Hoefer and Marion Stuart are good friends that we dine with quite often. Buz has helped me many times in the catering business. He is a retired guy, like me, and loves to cook and entertain. Marion makes this wonderful salad dressing that we have used many times in a catering venue. It's easy and works well, so well that we have made it by the gallon for several events.

1/3 cup olive oil
1/3 cup salad oil
1/3 cup red wine vinegar
1 teaspoon Jane's Crazy Salt
¼ teaspoon Italian Herb Seasoning
¼ teaspoon dry or prepared mustard
¼ teaspoon ground black pepper
Crushed garlic to taste

Prep time: 15 min.
Yield: Approx. 1 cup

Shake well and chill before use. Shake well before serving. This dressing is very versatile. It expands easily and it keeps well when refrigerated.

Poached Pears in Red Wine

This has become a standard with us for use in salad. Prior to this recipe Carol stuck with the Mandarin oranges. She found a recipe for poached pears and began tinkering with it. When she got it down her moniker as "Salad Maven" was guaranteed. They are fast, easy and quite good. They are best served chilled and work well in salads to provide a different texture. If you're wondering what else they are good for, our granddaughters love them for a snack.

4 large pears, peeled, cored and sliced
1 ½ cups dry red wine
1 cup sugar
1 2-inch strip of lemon zest
2 tablespoons fresh lemon juice
4 whole cloves
1 2-inch cinnamon stick

Prep time: About 30 min.
Yield: Enough for 8 salads

Combine the ingredients, except for the pears, in a saucepan and bring the mixture to a boil. Lower the heat and simmer covered until the sugar is dissolved. Place the pear slices in the simmering mixture and cook until tender, about 10 minutes. Let them cool in the syrup, still covered. If you don't use them right away, remove the cinnamon stick and cloves and refrigerate. They will keep in the refrigerator for several days.

Ceasar Salad

A few years ago, for our 30th anniversary, Carol and I decided to do something different to celebrate the occasion. We ended up in Freeport, Maine. How's that for different? Since we knew very little about the state we logged on to some sites on the Internet and did some reading. We kept getting drawn to what the natives call "Down East" Maine and more specifically to Freeport. There were a number of mentions of the Harraseeket Inn so we decided that we would check it out. What a find! This is an outstanding inn with the feel of a very nice, well-run bed and breakfast. It houses two excellent restaurants, one upscale with a wine list featured in Wine Spectator magazine and the other a little more relaxed with wood-fired ovens and grill. One evening we dined on an outstanding Chateaubriand served with a Ceasar Salad that was prepared tableside. They were kind enough to explain the process as they prepared the salad and I persevered in my attempts to emulate it long enough to make it taste like the tableside version. Like many other recipes, this one takes a little time to get the "feel" of it. My advice is to stay with it; the results are worth the effort. One thing I would mention is that I use pasteurized eggs for this dressing. You will find them in most grocery stores these days. I also suggest starting with a small lemon; you can always add more juice if needed.

1 lemon
1 teaspoon pureed anchovies
1 egg yolk
2 cloves pressed garlic
2 tablespoons olive oil
Parmigiano-Reggiano cheese, grated
Ground black pepper
Croutons
1 head Romaine lettuce

Prep time: 15 min.
Yield: 4 servings

Squeeze the juice of one lemon into a seasoned wooden salad bowl. Mix the pureed anchovies, egg yolk, black pepper and pressed garlic in the bowl with the lemon juice. Add the olive oil and mix well. Toss the lettuce in the bowl with the dressing and add the croutons. Sprinkle the grated Parmesan cheese on the salad and serve.

Classic Potato Salad

Like many other Southern dishes this one has as many variations as there are people preparing it. We found this one worked best for us in the catering business and we served it often with grilled burgers, brats or butterflied pork chop sandwiches. It was also a hit with the Grilled Cajun Style Stuffed Pork Loin when we served it. It is best when prepared well ahead of time and allowed to chill. We preferred to use Yukon Gold potatoes, however red potatoes worked well. As a rule we do not peel potatoes for this salad.

2 pounds medium potatoes
2 hardboiled eggs
¾ cup mayonnaise
1 tablespoon prepared mustard
½ cup sweet pickle relish, drained
1 small jar pimentos, drained
½ teaspoon salt
½ teaspoon pepper (fresh ground
   is preferred)
Paprika for garnish

Prep time: 1 hour
Yield: Approx. 12 servings

Place the potatoes in a pot with water to cover. Bring the water to a boil and reduce heat. Simmer, covered, for 20-25 minutes or until just tender. Drain well and cool slightly. Cube potatoes.

Boil eggs and separate yolks and whites. Coarsely chop the whites.

In a large mixing bowl combine the mayonnaise, mustard, mashed egg yolks, salt and pepper. Stir in the drained sweet pickle relish and pimentos. Add the cubed potatoes and coarsely chopped egg whites. Toss lightly to coat and test for seasoning. Chill for 6 to 24 hours. To serve, transfer salad to a serving bowl and garnish with paprika. This recipe serves about 12 and expands easily. We have made this up in batches as big as 40 pounds with excellent results.

Cole Slaw

Here's a recipe that is often taken for granted. Nobody seems to pay much attention to the cole slaw, unless it's not good. I classify coleslaw in two categories and I like both. One of the two types has a creamy base and the other is a vinegar base. We found the creamy base paired well with a savory grilled pork chop and the one featured here is particularly good with Fried Catfish and Hushpuppies. Because of that, this one saw a lot of action in the catering business. Anytime we served catfish and hush puppies this was an expected side dish. Plan ahead so the onions will have time to marinate in the vinegar and oil and the entire mixture will have sufficient time to chill.

1 pound shredded cabbage
½ cup sugar
½ cup apple cider vinegar
½ cup Canola oil
1 small onion coarsely chopped
1 teaspoon celery seed
1 teaspoon salt

Prep time: 15 min.
Yield: 10 servings

In a saucepan heat the sugar, celery seed, salt, oil, and vinegar until the sugar and salt have dissolved. Add the onions and place in the refrigerator for 2-3 hours until the mixture is cooled. About an hour before serving pour the dressing over the cabbage and mix well. Return to the refrigerator until ready to serve. This makes about 10 servings and expands easily. We usually mixed it up in 10-pound batches when we did a fish fry.

Fruit Salad

This is an easy, great tasting fruit salad that holds very well. It's versatile because you can use either fresh fruits when in season or a mix of canned and frozen fruits with excellent results. We had tried this before and had some problems keeping the bananas from turning dark before we served it. In talking with Amy, Brett's wife, she said she had used peach pie filling as a base for the salad and it worked well. Because the liquid in the peach pie filling coats the fruit, fresh bananas can be used and they won't turn brown. We've served this on several occasions at brunches for large groups of people.

1 pineapple, peeled, cored and cut into chunks
2 pints fresh strawberries, sliced
1 pint blueberries
3 bananas, cut into chunks
1 can peach pie filling
1 cup chopped pecans (optional)

Prep time: 20 min.
Yield: 10 servings

Place all of the fruits in a large bowl with the peach pie filling being the last addition. Stir gently to coat all of the fruit and chill until needed. This can be prepared well in advance to avoid the last minute rush. The pecans are optional but they do add a nice contrasting texture to the mix. This salad expands easily; however, if we are preparing a larger amount we will mix everything but the bananas the day before and wait until shortly before serving to cut and add the bananas.

More friends and family at the anniversary party

We're Rolling Now

Because there are so many great recipes that could be in this grouping I had a hard time determining just which ones to include. I finally resolved the crisis by establishing some benchmarks: how long had I been cooking it, how much tradition was embodied in it, the history of the recipe, and how easy it is to duplicate. I settled on the ones here knowing that there is another cookbook waiting to be written that would include many more. These are classics in my repertoire, many of which go back nearly 40 years.

88 ~ Catfish and Crawfish Breaux Bridge

89 ~ Cajun Style Stuffed Pork Chops

90 ~ Southern Fried Chicken

91 ~ Tim's Best Chicken, Sausage and Pork Jambalaya

92 ~ Deep Fried Turkey

93 ~ Crawfish Etouffee

94 ~ Chicken Cornelius

95 ~ Mom's Shrimp Creole

96 ~ Ben's Gobblin' Good Turkey

97 ~ Shrimp Curry

98 ~ New Orleans Style Red Beans and Rice

99 ~ Cajun Style Roasted Pork Loin

100 ~ Roast Beef Mom's Way

Catfish and Crawfish Breaux Bridge

When we moved from Alexandria, Louisiana to LaCrosse, Wisconsin it was more than just a job transfer. It was a leap in cultures from the South to the Midwest, from the Cajun influence of South Louisiana to the equally strong Scandinavian and German influence of the Midwest. Social differences notwithstanding, I must say the only real adaptation that we had to deal with was the lack of good fresh seafood that was so common in Louisiana. Carol and I and Brandon, the only one of our children left at home, dutifully became acquainted with the obligatory Friday night fish fry in Western Wisconsin. Batter fried cod is a huge leap from catfish rolled in seasoned cornmeal and deep-fried! We worked hard at it and found that if one sprinkles a little Tabasco on the cod it becomes passable fare.

Upon our departure from Alexandria, my wonderfully talented secretary, Margie Phillips, presented me with a beautifully assembled copy of all of the recipes that I had gathered at that time. The book is complete with watercolor drawings throughout, provided by a good friend of Margie's, and even has a section entitled "Mes Amis" that includes favorite recipes from members of the staff that worked with me. One of those recipes is from my friend Sid Broussard in Breaux Bridge, Louisiana and it inspired this offering. If you don't recognize the name of the town you need to be aware that this sleepy little Cajun town lights up every year and hosts the widely publicized Crawfish Festival. The crawfish, though not unique to the area, often is used as the popular symbol of all that is Cajun in Louisiana. I have never eaten crawfish from this region of the state that was not good. By the way, we have found that WalMart in LaCrosse, Wisconsin stocks frozen crawfish tails! Now that's a find!

Largely because of the long cold Wisconsin winters I have had to develop some adaptations from the original version. Brandon and I further adapted this recipe for use in the catering business and served it many times. This recipe provides some interesting contrasts in tastes and texture and it proved to be a real treat for those who ordered it.

6 catfish filets
1 pound crawfish tails
1 can cream of mushroom soup
1 large onion
1 large bell pepper
1 stick unsalted butter
Celebration Seasonings Cajun Style All Purpose Seasoning Blend, to taste

Prep time: 30 min.
Cook time: 40 min.
Yield: 6 servings

Sauté the crawfish, diced onion and bell pepper in a heavy pot on the stove. Season to taste with Celebration Seasonings Cajun Style All Purpose Seasoning Blend. When the onions are wilted, pour in one can of cream of mushroom soup with an equal amount of water. Stir this mixture well, cover the pan and simmer for twenty minutes. Roll the catfish in seasoned cornmeal and pan-fry it to a golden brown. Most often I pan fry the catfish first and hold it in a 170° oven. It will stay crispy and not dry out while you cook the crawfish sauce.

To serve, ladle the sauce over the filet and garnish with the parsley flakes. I sometimes cook rice and serve some of the sauce over rice alongside of the fish. It's great with a green salad and crusty French bread.

Cajun Style Stuffed Pork Chops

As mentioned elsewhere in this book, when we were living in Lafayette, Louisiana we used to shop at a meat market named Veron's Shopping Block. They specialized in Cajun meats that were the best I've ever had. Their most notable offering was the sausage-stuffed pork chop. The recipe for this sausage is included in the breakfast section of this book. The chop was stuffed, seasoned and sold ready to cook. They were best slow cooked on the grill but they weren't bad cooked in the oven either. For years I've wanted to duplicate these pork chops but for a multitude of reasons (none of them very good) I just never got around to it. Around January 2000, I ran across a recipe for pure pork sausage that looked like it might work. With the addition of a couple of spices, the first attempt was so good that I wrote it down just as it was. As a breakfast sausage it is great. Made into links, it is so close to what I remember about Veron's that my first taste of it sent me back 30 years. The real test was the stuffed pork chop and it passed beautifully.

6 thick-cut pork chops
1 pound of pork sausage (recipe in
    Let The Good Times Begin section)
*Celebration Seasonings Cajun Style
    Seasoning Blend,* to taste

Prep time: 30 min.
Cook time: 1 hour
Yield: 6 servings

To stuff the pork chops load up the sausage stuffer just as you would to make links. Lay the pork chop flat on the chopping block. With a sharp filet knife cut an incision in the edge of the pork chop of sufficient size to allow you to insert the sausage stuffer into it. Work the knife from right to left to cut a pocket inside of the chop. Insert the stuffer in the pocket and fill the pocket with sausage. When you withdraw the stuffer there should be only about a one inch incision showing on the edge of the chop. If you don't have a sausage stuffer cut the chop along the edge as though you were butterflying it. Once cut in this fashion, place the sausage stuffing in the center and fold the chop back over and secure it with a toothpick, if necessary. Season the pork chop with Celebration Seasonings Cajun Style All Purpose Seasoning Blend and slow cook it on the grill or in the oven. I use two or three ounces of sausage per pork chop. This is an outstanding main dish and pairs well with several of our side dishes, most notably Corn a l'Acadien and/or Dirty Rice.

Southern Fried Chicken

I don't know when Carol came up with this recipe. It was a long time ago. I really believe all Southern women come programmed with certain recipes and this is one of them. It's great and never fails to be a crowd pleaser. Several years ago, during a particularly long winter, we decided to have a party in February. We invited about twenty people over and had a wintertime picnic. Carol fried six chickens and made Apple Baked Beans and a Classic Potato Salad. We all sat around a big fire in the fireplace and acted like it was summertime! That's the only part that was difficult, since it was around 15 degrees outside! If there is any chicken left over it holds well in the refrigerator.

2 frying chickens, cut up, washed,
    drained and patted dry
2 cups buttermilk
3 eggs
Seasoned flour for dredging
1 Chicken-frying skillet
Hot oil to cover halfway up the side
    of the chicken pieces
2-3 cups milk
*Celebration Seasonings Cajun Style
    All Purpose Seasoning Blend*

Prep time: 1 hr.
Cook time: 1 hr.
Yield: 16 pieces

Season the chicken with *Celebration Seasonings Cajun Style All Purpose Seasoning Blend* and set aside. Beat the eggs and blend them with the buttermilk. Place the pieces of cut up chicken in the buttermilk-egg mixture and marinate for about 20 minutes. When ready to fry the chicken heat the oil to 350°. Dredge the chicken pieces in the seasoned flour and fry until the juices run clear when you poke the chicken with a fork. Otherwise, a meat thermometer works quite well. The internal temperature of the cooked chicken should be 165°. Drain the chicken and place in a 170° oven to hold. When all the chicken is done, drain all but 3 or 4 tablespoons of the oil and leave the bits of batter and chicken in the pan. Add about ¼ to ½ cup of flour to the pan and stir until browned. Add milk as needed and stir until the gravy has the desired consistency. Season to taste. Serve this gravy over mashed potatoes or *Tim's Never Fail Lighter Than Air Buttermilk Biscuits.*

Tim's Best Chicken, Sausage and Pork Jambalaya

Jambalaya, like gumbo, is one of those dishes that everybody claims to have some secret ingredient for or some process that is uniquely theirs. Many are reluctant to share this information and hold it as a family secret. Well, my secret is out and it is really no secret at all, its just very good jambalaya. This recipe is the result of many years of cooking for hundreds of people. This lengthy evolution has made allowances for every possible shortcut and time saving step as well as the most consistent blending of ingredients. It would be safe to say it has been distilled to its essence. This basic recipe makes 16 cups of jambalaya. We usually allow 2 cups for a serving and rarely ever serve that much. With a few notable exceptions, folks just don't eat that much. As information, 2 cups of this jambalaya weighs 1 pound! This recipe expands easily and we've cooked it for as many as 350 people. It was one of the most requested entrees from our catering menu and I don't ever remember hearing a complaint about this dish.

1 lb. sausage, cut into bite-sized pieces
1 lb. pork, cut into ¼ inch cubes
1 lb. chicken, de-boned and cut into bite-sized pieces
3 stalks celery, diced
1 medium bell pepper, diced
1 medium onion, diced
4 cloves garlic, crushed or at the very least finely diced
1½ cups crushed tomatoes in puree
4½ cups chicken stock
3 cups of raw converted rice (I use *Uncle Ben's*)
Celebration Seasonings Cajun Style All-Purpose Seasoning Blend, to taste
1 bunch of green onions, finely diced

Prep time: 45 min.
Cook time 1 hour
Yield: 8 servings

Brown the pork in a large heavy pot, preferably cast iron, until it begins to caramelize. Season the meat as it is cooking. When browned remove from the pot and set aside. Add the chicken and cook until the meat begins to stick to the bottom again. Season the chicken as it is cooking. When done, remove from the pot and set aside. Add the sausage and cook in the same fashion. Because the sausage is generally well seasoned, it is not necessary to season it now. When the sausage is browned, remove it from the pot and set aside. Now add the diced celery, bell pepper, onion and crushed garlic and cook until the veggies begin to sweat. The vegetable juices will loosen the bits of meat stuck to the pot. Scrape the pot to get all of the bits and pieces free, and stir the mixture well. Add all of the cooked meat back to the pot and stir well. Now add the mixture of crushed tomatoes in puree and chicken stock and stir well. Test the seasoning and if necessary season to taste with *Celebration Seasonings Cajun Style All-Purpose Seasoning Blend* and let simmer for 30 or more minutes. Test again for seasoning and adjust as necessary. Stir in the raw rice and cover the pot tightly. In about 10 minutes, lift the lid and gently turn the rice mixture over to keep it from sticking. Cover tightly and cook until done, about another 15 minutes. Serve with green salad and good toasted garlic bread.

Deep Fried Turkey

This now popular method of cooking turkey began to get some press in South Louisiana in the late 70's and early 80's. We were living in Lake Charles, Louisiana when I started to hear about it and I was intrigued. It wasn't a common practice at the time so I was left to my own devices to figure out how to do it. That was a long time before turkey frying pots and outdoor burners were widely available at sporting goods stores and hardware stores. How I figured it all out is kind of a long story and if we ever meet, ask me about it and I'll tell all! Suffice it to say, I worked it out and here are the results. Since that time we have cooked hundreds of turkeys and in the catering business once fried 93 in one day! Check out the picture section to see the pot we used. As a matter of interest, Cornish hens work very well this way and we have fried as many as 35 at a time. They are quick and easy and don't require carving, other than to cut them in half for serving. They cook in about 20 minutes!

1 Turkey frying pot and an outdoor propane burner
Peanut oil, sufficient to cover the turkey and leave
    some freeboard in the pot to allow for splashing
1 10-12 pound turkey, thawed
½ stick butter, melted
1½ teaspoons garlic powder
1 tablespoon Worcestershire Sauce
2 teaspoons lemon juice
*Celebration Seasonings Cajun Style All Purpose
    Seasoning Blend,* to taste

Prep time: 30 min.
Cook time: Approx 45 min.
Yield: 10 servings

Please thaw the turkey before putting it in the oil. If dropped in a pot of hot oil, a frozen turkey will cause an explosion! Don't laugh; people have done it! Melt the butter and blend in the other ingredients. Inject this mixture in the turkey breast, thighs and legs. Coat the outside with *Celebration Seasonings Cajun Style All Purpose Seasoning Blend* and place in the refrigerator for several hours or overnight. When ready to cook, heat the oil to 350° and slowly immerse the turkey into the oil. Be careful to avoid splashing any hot oil on yourself. I use welder's gloves for this step. The rule of thumb is that it takes about 3 minutes per pound to thoroughly cook the turkey. Don't rely on this, use a meat thermometer and cook the turkey to an internal temperature of 165°. I would suggest buying one of the long stem thermometers now available to check the temperature of the oil. If you aren't careful the oil will overheat and the outside of the turkey will burn, leaving the inside not properly cooked. When the turkey is done tent it with aluminum foil and let it rest about 15 minutes before carving. The temperature will rise another 5 to 10 degrees. Carve and serve. This feeds approximately 10 people very well with some left for Turkey Bone Soup (see recipe in The Warm Up section). Fried turkey pairs well with any combination of Corn a l'Acadien, Dirty Rice, Apple Baked Beans and Classic Potato Salad. Here's a carving tip: Cut the whole breast halves off of the turkey and lay them on a chopping block. Cut each breast across the grain and they will stay together and be easier to serve.

Crawfish Etouffee

This is a simple, yet classic crawfish recipe. As I have read, its origin was in the kitchen of a small hotel in downtown Breaux Bridge, Louisiana, the Crawfish Capital of the world and the home of the famous Crawfish Festival. This is a festival that routinely has folks backed up for miles on Interstate 10 just to get into town. The festival has been around for a long time and it would seem that anything having to do with crawfish and the consumption of crawfish could have no better pedigree than to lay claim to having originated in Breaux Bridge. Like so many Cajun recipes there are variations "out the wazoo!" That doesn't mean they are all good and in fact, some are just plain bad. This recipe, which is derived from the original, does not call for a roux. However, various outstanding chefs over the years have added a roux with some good results. Some use a light roux with butter and flour and others use a traditional roux with oil and flour. Each type brings a different taste to the table. I prefer the version written here with no roux as a stand-alone entrée served over cooked white rice. You may substitute shrimp for crawfish if the latter is not available. It will be good but the shrimp does not have as distinctive a taste as the crawfish. That would be an instance where I would use 2-3 tablespoons of roux to enhance the dish. As information, "Etouffee" means to smother.

4 pounds crawfish tails
½ pound butter
2 medium onions, diced
3 stalks celery, finely diced
½ large bell pepper
4 cloves garlic
2 tablespoons cornstarch
3 cups water
Celebration Seasonings Cajun Style All Purpose Seasoning Blend, to taste

Prep time: 30 min.
Cook time: 45 min.
Yield: 10 servings

Season the crawfish with *Celebration Seasonings Cajun Style All Purpose Seasoning Blend* and set aside. Sauté onions, celery, bell pepper and garlic in the butter. Add the crawfish and simmer for about 20 minutes. Dissolve cornstarch in the water and add to the mixture. Cook until thick, stirring occasionally. Test for seasoning and serve over cooked rice with a green salad and good garlic bread. This recipe serves 10.

Chicken Cornelius

This is one of my all time favorite recipes. The sauce in this dish is so good it must be sinful. It's easy to prepare and is always a hit. We got the recipe from old friends Chuck and Hazel Gahagan in Lake Charles, Louisiana. As I recall, it had been published in Southern Living magazine. In it's original form it called for the breast to be cooked with the rib cage intact. Over time we have found this dish easier to cook, serve and eat if the breast is de-boned and skinless. We have also found that the recipe can be expanded without necessarily expanding the sauce proportions. On a couple of occasions I've cooked this for staff retreats and have had people re-heat the left over sauce to eat with their biscuits the next morning!

Becky Neimeir and Kevin Murphy, two classmates of our son, Brandon, got married in the summer of 1999 and as a gift to them we catered their rehearsal dinner for 40 people. We served this dish along with steamed green beans, mashed Yukon Gold potatoes and Mom's Rolls, found in the Bread section of this book. They left nothing. It was the easiest clean up we have ever done. Here's the recipe.

7 de-boned skinless chicken breasts
1 can cream of mushroom soup
1 can cream of chicken soup
1 pint whipping cream
1 cup dry vermouth
Celebration Seasonings Cajun Style
    All Purpose Seasoning Blend
2 cups sliced fresh mushrooms

Prep time: 20 min.
Cook time: 1 hour
Yield: 7 servings

Season the chicken breasts with *Celebration Seasonings Cajun Style All Purpose Seasoning Blend*. Place the breasts in a deep baking pan. Whisk together the two cans of soup, the whipping cream and the cup of vermouth. Pour this over the seasoned chicken breasts and bake at 350° for one hour. Sauté the mushrooms and serve over the dish. This is excellent served with mashed potatoes and several different steamed green vegetables such as green beans, asparagus or broccoli. As mentioned above this recipe expands easily and can feed a large crowd.

Mom's Shrimp Creole

There's Shrimp Creole and then there's Mom's Shrimp Creole. As I've mentioned elsewhere in this book, characteristically, Mom never wrote down any recipes. If one of her children didn't call her and get the first hand word of mouth recipe and subsequently write it down, it never got written. When I called my brother, Steve, and asked if he had Mom's recipe for Shrimp Creole his first question was, "Was there one ever written?" That was a bad omen, because if neither of us had it there was only one shot left. I felt certain Dianne, my sister, probably had it written, but I also knew she has moved several times and might not be able to locate it. I was delighted to get a call from her when she heard I was looking for that recipe. Dianne had stood by the stove and watched Mom cook it way back when she first got married and still had the original copy with a few tomato stains on it to attest to its authenticity. I had always felt sure it had a couple of "secret" steps in it because I've eaten Shrimp Creole for a lifetime and never had one taste just like Mom's. Here's the original and I'm sorry it took me so long to resurrect it. I have taken the liberty of adding the use of *Celebration Seasonings Cajun Style All Purpose Seasoning Blend* to the recipe. Is that literary license or something?

2 pounds shrimp
½ cup oil
1 cup flour
1 large onion
2 medium bell peppers
2-3 stalks celery
1 large clove garlic
½ cup green onions
½ cup parsley
2 small cans tomato paste (Mom said Contadina Tomato Paste)
1 small can tomato sauce
1 can V8 juice (one of the secrets)
Water, as needed
3 tablespoons Worcestershire sauce (the other secret)
1 pinch sugar
Celebration Seasonings Cajun Style All Purpose Seasoning Blend
1 tablespoon thyme
2 bay leaves

Prep time: 30 min.
Cook time: 1 1/2 hrs
Yield: 8 servings

I know a lot of smart people who say you shouldn't cook a tomato-based dish in a cast iron pot. I do it anyway. Mom always cooked this in a big cast iron pot, which by the way is still in the family. I think Steve has it. Start by using 1 cup of flour and ½ cup oil to make a roux in that big pot. This will be a fairly thick roux. When it is a nice dark brown add the diced onion, bell peppers, celery and garlic and cook until the onions are wilted. Add the tomato paste and cook for several minutes until the paste is dark. Add the tomato sauce, the V8 and water as needed to make a thick mixture. Add the seasonings to taste, cover and cook for about 45 minutes. Add the parsley and green onion and cook uncovered for another 5-10 minutes. Taste for seasoning and add the shrimp. Cook uncovered for another 10 minutes and serve over rice with a green salad and good garlic bread. That's it...enjoy!

Ben's Gobblin' Good Turkey

When I was working in the Century Telephone Company organization I had occasion to work with the late Bennie Walker. He was from Greensburg, a little hamlet in Southeastern Louisiana. Like many men in Louisiana, Bennie was a master hunter and fine cook. He had studied and hunted wild turkeys for many years. He believed you shouldn't kill anything if you didn't have any intention of cooking and eating it. To that end, he had devised this great recipe for cooking wild turkey breast. Actually, it is quite good when prepared with "store bought" turkey breast. This is a rather easy recipe to prepare and is excellent served over linguine. We've cooked it many times and I never fail to think of Bennie when we sit down to eat. I have taken the liberty of substituting our own seasoning blend for the seasonings he had originally suggested.

4 filets of turkey breast
8 tablespoons unsalted butter
1 cup green onions
½ pound mushrooms
Celebration Seasonings Cajun Style All Purpose Blend, to taste
¼ cup apple brandy (white wine works also)
4 tablespoons whipping cream

Prep time: 30 min.
Cook time: 30 min.
Yield: 4 servings

On a cutting board, pound filets with a meat tenderizer. Season the tenderized meat and lightly dust with flour. Brown the meat slowly in 4 tablespoons of unsalted butter. Remove the meat from the skillet and set aside in a 170° oven. Melt the remaining butter in the skillet and when the foam dissipates, add chopped green onions to the skillet and sauté lightly. Add ¼ cup apple brandy or white wine and cook until the mixture begins to thicken. Add the mushrooms and sauté until shrinking is observed in the mushrooms. Add 4 tablespoons of whipping cream and stir to incorporate the cream. When the sauce has thickened test for seasoning. To serve place the turkey on the dish with the linguine and ladle the sauce over both.

Shrimp Curry

Once while visiting Carol's parents in El Dorado, Arkansas we were invited to dinner at the home of their close friends Joe and Gwen Haas. The menu that evening was to be shrimp curry served over rice. Carol and I had never eaten this dish and were pleasantly surprised at how good it was and how simple it was to cook. At least it was simple until Gwen started to cook the rice! She rinsed the rice first and then put it into the pot covered with water. She then placed it on a burner and turned the heat up. When the rice started to cook she removed the pot from the heat, drained the rice and then rinsed it again. Then she put some amount of water back in the pot with the rice and cooked it. The rice turned out good but I don't recall ever seeing anybody torture rice that much when cooking it and I've seen a lot it of done! Lately, when cooking this curry dish I've been using a "hot" curry from Penzey's Spices that is excellent. Try it for a different taste.

3 pounds peeled and deviened shrimp
3 tablespoons butter
1 ½ cups finely chopped onion
2 tablespoons curry powder
2 cans cream of shrimp soup
1 cup milk
1 cup sour cream
4 cups cooked rice

Prep time: 20 min.
Cook time: 1 hr.
Yield: 8 servings

Sauté onions in butter, add curry powder and mix well. Remove from heat and blend in milk and shrimp soup. Cook slowly until hot. Stir constantly because this mixture has a tendency to stick. Add shrimp and cook 15 minutes. Once again, do not allow mixture to boil; there is plenty enough heat to cook shrimp without getting it that hot. If you allow it to get too hot now you can scorch the whole affair and shrimp are just too expensive to throw away. Just before serving blend in the sour cream. Serve over rice. This is great with a green salad and toasted garlic bread.

New Orleans Style Red Beans and Rice

We didn't eat a lot of red beans and rice when I was growing up, but we did have pinto and navy beans. The basis for cooking all of these beans is about the same in Louisiana. The biggest difference is the addition of sausage to the red beans. The use of red beans is a New Orleans tradition that goes back to the days of the housewives cooking beans on Monday while they were doing the wash. The beans cooked slowly and didn't need a lot of tending, which made them a perfect dish for washday. If Cajun Andouille sausage is available it is preferred, but I have used Polish sausage, smoked sausage or both with equal success. This dish, in some variation, is found on just about every Monday lunch menu in the city of New Orleans. Probably one of the best examples we ever found, and we went back regularly for quality assurance purposes, was at a little hole in the wall restaurant on the docks in New Orleans. They made and sold boatloads of red beans. The smell of those beans, cooked until the gravy was a soft and creamy pink, spiked with a hot smoked sausage and chased with a Barq's Root Beer would bring the toughest dockhand back to his mother's table. We used to observe an unbeliev-able cross section of the population in this place. From suits to street people, it was like a religious experience, if only for a short time, at midday on Monday.

1 pound red kidney beans (I have used small red beans with excellent results)
1 cup chopped onion
1 cup chopped bell pepper
4 cloves minced garlic
3 stalks diced celery
1 bunch minced green onion tops
1 pound cubed ham
1 pound sliced Andouille, smoked sausage or polish sausage
Cooked white rice
Celebration Seasonings Cajun Style All Purpose Seasoning Blend, to taste

Prep time: 30 min.
Cook time: Approx. 2 hours
Yield: 12 generous servings

Rinse the beans and set aside to soak in water overnight or for at least four hours. Combine the diced onion, bell pepper, garlic and celery and set aside. Mince the green onions and set aside in a separate bowl. Combine the ham and the sausage and pre-fry in a large pot. When the meat starts to stick add the onions, bell pepper, garlic and celery mixture and sauté until the onions are wilted and the pot is deglazed. Be sure to scrape the pot to loosen all of the browned bits of meat. Add 4 cups of water and cook this mixture for about fifteen minutes or until it is well blended. Add the drained beans and sufficient water to cover the beans by about two inches. Cook over low heat with the cover askew until the beans are tender. Season to taste with Celebration Seasonings Cajun Style All Purpose Seasoning Blend. When testing for doneness, adjust the seasoning as necessary. Before serving sprinkle the green onions on top of the beans and serve the beans over cooked rice. This meal is tra-ditionally served with garlic bread but Mom's Corn-bread (found in the You Have To Have A Little Dough section) is a great match with the red beans as well.

Cajun Style Roasted Pork Loin

I can't even begin to guess how many pounds of this pork loin I've prepared. The number would be in the big hundreds. It was a huge hit on our catering menu and was one of our most requested dishes. It pairs beautifully with Dirty Rice and Corn a l'Acadien. This pork loin cooks wonderfully in the oven and with some modifications can easily be cooked on the grill.

Seasoning Mix

5½ teaspoons *Celebration Seasonings*
  All Purpose Cajun Style Seasoning Blend
1 teaspoon sweet paprika
1 teaspoon dried thyme leaves
½ teaspoon dry mustard
4 tablespoons unsalted butter
½ cup finely diced onion
½ cup finely diced celery
½ cup finely diced green bell pepper
1 tablespoon minced garlic
1 (4-pound) boneless pork loin

Prep time: 30 min.
Cook time: 1½ – 2 hours
Yield: 8 8-oz. servings

Thoroughly combine the seasoning mix ingredients. Melt the butter in a deep skillet and stir in the seasoning mix. Place all chopped vegetables in the butter/seasoning mix and sauté about 4 minutes over high heat, stirring occasionally. Cool.

Meanwhile, place the roast in a baking pan, fat side up. With a sharp knife make several deep slits across the grain in the meat to form pockets, being careful not to cut through to the bottom. Stuff the pockets with the vegetable/seasoning mixture, and then thoroughly rub the remaining mixture over the entire roast by hand.

Bake uncovered at 275° for about 1 to 1½ hours or until the internal temperature is 135°, then at 425° until dark brown on top and meat is white in center. This should take about 10 to 15 minutes more or until the internal temperature is 145°. Take the meat out and let it rest for about 10-15 minutes before slicing.

When preparing this dish on the grill, I butterfly the whole loin and spread the stuffing inside the opened loin and then truss it with cook's twine. This keeps the stuffing from falling out when turned on the grill. Be careful; it doesn't take as long to cook on the grill. Watch for flare-ups. Be guided by the internal temperature.

Roast Beef Mom's Way

I've only recently written this recipe down and I can't tell you how many times it has been served in our household. Roast beef, rice and gravy and English peas sounds like a lunch menu that most folks, at least in our part of the world, associate with their youth. To us it is a traditional Sunday lunch ranking right up there with Southern Fried Chicken and Mashed Potatoes. I can never eat roast beef without going back to the days, as the Southern colloquialism so aptly puts it, of having my feet under Dad's table and eating Mom's cooking. I favor about a five pound rump roast for this. That's more than is needed for a normal family meal, but let's not forget that roast beef sandwiches for a weekday lunch are quite good. One other noteworthy item in this recipe is the use of a cast iron Dutch oven with a tight fitting lid. I have a large collection of cast iron cookware and have written a section in the book on the benefits, use and care of this wonderful old time cookware.

1 5-pound rump roast
2-3 cloves garlic
Flour for dredging
salt and pepper to taste

Prep time: 20 min.
Cook time: 2-2½ hrs.
Yield: 8-10 servings

Preheat the oven to 325°. Peel the garlic and slice it into several thin pieces. With a sharp knife, pierce the roast and slide a slice of garlic down the blade as deep into the roast as you can. Continue this all around the roast until you have used all of the garlic. Next, pierce the roast with the knife and spread the slit open to allow for salt to be poured into the opening. Make the incisions for the salt around the roast as you did for the garlic. Mix salt and pepper with the flour and dredge the roast in this mixture. Pour 2-3 tablespoons of oil in the bottom of the pot and heat it on the stovetop. When hot, place the roast in the pot and brown it on all sides. Once this is done pour a cup of water in the pot, place the lid on tightly and put it in the oven. After about 1 hour of cooking time, open the pot and pour in enough water to bring the level of the water about 2 inches up the side of the roast. Replace the lid and continue cooking until the roast is fully cooked, about another 30-45 minutes. Test for doneness with a thermometer. This roast is best when fork tender, which is about 175°. When done, remove the roast and thicken the gravy, testing for seasoning. Slice the roast and serve with cooked white rice. This is a sensational main dish.

Carol and Tim at Stowe, Vermont celebrating after the anniversary party

The Supporting Cast

If I were to write a definition of a side dish it would probably read something like this: "A complementary dish, typically a vegetable, to be served with an entrée." However, some of our side dishes are so good that it's hard to keep them from stealing the show. One such dish is the Corn a l'Acadien. It is unusual to ever have any of this left over, regardless of how much you prepare. It is so unique, certainly in this part of the country, and so good, guests just can't seem to get enough of it. Try it out and you'll see what I mean. In the catering business we found that many of our side dishes had the same effect, perhaps because they were so different from normal fare. Whatever the case, every one of the recipes in this group is well-proven. We've successfully served them many times and have never failed to receive accolades. I intentionally did not include basic recipes like steamed vegetables, macaroni and cheese and various other recipes that can be found in a million or so other cookbooks. The ones I included are of a different cast that feature some wonderful flavors and textures.

Corn a l'Acadien (Cajun Corn)

This is an incredible side dish! One evening I was invited to a cook out organized by our work group in Ville Platte, Louisiana. It was at a fishing camp on a bayou outside of town. We had a wonderful meal prepared by several of the men in the group. For the life of me, I can't remember for sure what the main dish was that night. I think it was grillades, strips of lean beef braised in rich brown gravy served over rice. A side dish of corn was added along with a good green salad. I remember the main dish being very good but it was the corn that stole the show. I had never seen corn fixed the way it was that evening. This is an original.

It became a standard side dish in the catering business and it went with just about anything. It is excellent with barbecue, deep fried turkey, or any kind of pork. By request I have also served it as a side with Chicken, Sausage and Pork Jambalaya. Even though that was not my favorite combination, everybody else loved it! Here's the recipe.

1 pound smoked sausage
1 medium onion, diced
1 medium bell pepper, diced
2 stalks celery, diced
2 green onions, finely diced
2½ pounds frozen whole kernel corn
Celebration Seasonings Cajun Style
*   All Purpose Seasoning Blend,* to taste

Prep time: 30 min.
Cook time: 30 min.
Yield: Approx. 10 servings

Dice the onion, bell pepper and celery and set aside. Finely dice the green onion and set aside.

Cut the sausage in half lengthwise and then cut each half in half lengthwise. Now cut the strips of sausage into bits so that when finished you have small quarter rounds. Brown the sausage in a heavy cast iron pot until it begins to caramelize. Add the chopped veggies and cook until the onions are translucent and the mixture becomes dark from the deglazing of the pot. Add the corn last and cook until hot. Season to taste with Celebration Seasonings Cajun Style All Purpose Seasoning Blend and garnish with finely diced green onions.

Dirty Rice (Rice Dressing)

This dish is quite likely one of the premier side dishes in the Cajun repertoire. We have catered it for some very large groups and it has always received high acclaim. I must admit that the traditional version of this dish is made with chicken giblets rather than ground beef and pork. Because we were doing missionary work, cooking Cajun food in the Midwest, we went with a mix that was a little less avant-garde and likely more acceptable for the Midwestern palate.

¾ pound lean ground beef
¾ pound ground pork
2 tablespoons canola oil
3-4 stalks celery, diced
1 medium bell pepper, diced
1 medium onion, diced
2 cloves garlic, crushed
4½ cups cooked rice (1½ cups of raw
   rice =4½ cups cooked)
Celebration Seasonings Cajun Style
   All Purpose Seasoning Blend, to taste
4 green onions, finely diced and set aside

Prep time: 30 min.
Cook time: 39 min.
Yield: 12 servings

Heat the canola oil in a heavy-bottomed pot, preferably a large cast iron Dutch oven. Crumble the ground beef and pork together and brown in the hot oil. When the meat is well browned and it is beginning to stick to the bottom of the pot, add the celery, bell pepper and onion. Cook until the onion is wilted. Add the crushed garlic and cook another 5 minutes. Season the mixture generously with Celebration Seasonings Cajun Style All-Purpose Seasoning Blend to taste. Add the cooked rice and mix well with the meat mixture. Garnish with the finely diced green onion and serve as a side dish with Deep Fried Turkey, Cajun Style Pork Loin or any good barbecue. It pairs well as a side dish with the Cajun Corn.

Crawfish Boudin

This is a fabulous side dish. Typically, boudin is stuffed in a casing and sold as part of a "Cajun" seven-course meal (that would be a six-pack of Budweiser and a pound of boudin). We began to see a few menus popping up that used Boudin as a side dish so we thought we would give it a try. One Friday night at our weekly fish fry, Brandon presented Roasted Cornish Hens stuffed with Crawfish Boudin as the special of the week. We roasted about a dozen Cornish hens and sold almost all of them. I was delighted we had some leftovers...they were great! The concept is no different than using traditional rice dressing as a side dish; however, these flavors are a little more intense. This dish pairs well with Pan Fried Catfish and Roasted or Deep Fried Cornish Hens, just to name two.

12 ounces frozen crawfish tails
Celebration Seasonings Cajun Style All Purpose Seasoning Blend, to taste
  (I would start with 1½ teaspoons)
2 tablespoons canola oil
2 cloves garlic, minced
½ cup green onions, finely diced
3 tablespoons flat leaf parsley, finely diced
1½ cups cooked rice

Prep time 30 min.
Cook time: 30 min.
Yield: 8 servings

The frozen crawfish are cooked when you buy them. When thawed, place them in a bowl and sprinkle the *Celebration Seasonings Cajun Style All Purpose Seasoning Blend* on top. Mix this well and set aside. Heat the canola oil and sauté the onions and garlic in a pan over medium-low heat for about 5 minutes. Stir in the green onions, parsley and crawfish and cook about 20 minutes more, stirring occasionally. Remove from the heat and thoroughly mix in the rice. Test for seasoning, which in this case means sample the wares, because I don't think you'll need to season it any more.

Apple Baked Beans

Oh, boy! Are these good beans! They're out of the ordinary because they aren't pinto beans or "pinks" which are the commonly used varieties for baked beans. Carol found the basic recipe on the side of a jar of Randall's Great Northern Beans and worked some magic on it to make it suit our taste. We served these in the catering business and I can't even guess how many times it was requested. The last time we served them was at a large wedding party and we prepared 10 gallons of them! They work well with Cajun Stuffed Pork Loin, Barbecued Ribs, Deep Fried Turkey and Southern Fried Chicken, just to name a few complementary main dishes. If you aren't careful, they'll upstage the main dish.

1 48-oz jar of Randall Great Northern Beans or the equivalent, drained and rinsed
3-4 strips bacon
3 cups of Granny Smith Apples, peeled and cubed
½ cup chopped onions
¾ cup light brown sugar, packed
½ cup ketchup
1 teaspoon cinnamon
1 teaspoon salt, or to taste

Prep time: 30 min.
Cook time: 1½ hrs. in all
Yield: 8 servings

Preheat the oven to 375°. Fry the bacon strips, crumble and set aside. Drain all but 2-3 tablespoons of the bacon grease. Place the onions in the same skillet and cook about 5 minutes. Add the apples and cook for about 10 minutes or until the apple cubes are tender. The juice from the onions and apples will deglaze the skillet. Scrape the skillet to break loose all the bits of stuck bacon caramelized on the bottom. Stir lightly to avoid crushing the apple cubes. In a large bowl mix together the brown sugar, ketchup, cinnamon and salt. Into this mixture, add the drained and rinsed beans and the reserved bacon and stir well. Add the contents of the skillet to this and mix well. Spray the sides of a 2-quart casserole with Pam and pour the entire mixture into it. Bake for 1 hour or until hot. This can be prepared well ahead of time and held in the refrigerator until time to cook. Make sure to heat it all the way through if you've held it in the refrigerator. An instant read thermometer should read 170° when the dish is ready.

Mixed Vegetable Stir Fry

It doesn't get any easier than this. This recipe accents the freshness of the vegetables that are used. It combines some great tastes and textures and with a little bit of help it takes on a new identity. Every once in a while I find myself just having to have a "fix" of some fresh vegetables fixed a little bit differently. Here it is.

½ pound broccoli florets
½ pound cauliflower florets
½ pound asparagus spears broken in two
1 red bell pepper, julienned
1 medium onion, cut in half and sliced
2 tablespoons of Grapeseed Oil or
    Peanut oil (either one has a high
    smoke point)
*Celebration Seasonings Cajun Style
All Purpose Seasoning Blend*

Prep time: 20 min.
Cook time: 10 min.
Yield: 8 servings

Prepare the vegetables and have them ready. This doesn't take long. I use a cast iron wok but any heavy bottomed skillet will work. Heat the oil until it is just about to smoke; if you have a laser thermometer that would be about 375°. Add the vegetables and stir-fry until the onions are beginning to wilt. At this point the other veggies should still be al dente. Now sprinkle the mixture lightly with the Celebration Seasonings Cajun Style All Purpose Seasoning Blend and toss to coat. Not too much seasoning, just enough to give it a little taste. The seasoning will light up those veggies! What a treat.

Wild Rice Pilaf

I love wild rice. The texture and the nutty taste bring a whole new dimension to a rice pilaf. I was looking for a side dish to serve with steak, grilled pork chops or grilled chicken breast and this one filled the bill.

We're talking easy here. Cook the wild rice ahead of time because it takes about 45 minutes to do so. Dice everything up ahead of time and have it set aside when you're ready to start this step of your menu. This doesn't take long to assemble so allow about 10 minutes.

2 cups cooked wild rice
½ cup celery, diced
6 green onions, finely diced, separate
    the green tops from the white bottoms
1 medium onion, diced
½ cup parched pecan pieces
Salt and pepper to taste
2-3 tablespoons unsalted butter

Prep time: 15 min.
Cook time: 1 hr. in all
Yield: 6-8 servings

Cook the wild rice according to the instructions on the manufacturer's package. In a cast iron skillet melt the unsalted butter and sauté the celery, onions and the white bottoms of the green onions. When the onions have wilted stir in the pecan pieces and the cooked wild rice and cook until hot. When ready to serve garnish the pilaf with the finely diced green onion tops. Serve as a side dish with steak, pork or chicken.

Cranberry-Apple Crisp

I guess cranberries, in some form, are an obligatory holiday side dish. However, you have to admit the customary cranberry sauce or cranberry jelly certainly lacks imagination. Well, here's a twist for you, pair that cranberry sauce with apples and you get a great contrast in taste. Our daughter-in-law Abby came through with this recipe as a side dish for Thanksgiving Dinner. For my money, with a little bit of whipped cream or ice cream as a topping, this is a great anytime dessert and we have served it as such. Sweet and tart, it does not have an overpowering sugary taste. If you want something different try it out.

1 can cranberry sauce
2 Granny Smith apple, peeled, cored and sliced thinly
1 cup oats
1 cup flour
1 cup brown sugar
¼ teaspoon baking powder
¼ teaspoon baking soda
½ cup softened butter

Prep time: 20 min
Cook time: 45 min
Yield: 8 servings

Preheat the oven to 350°. Sift the flour, baking powder and baking soda together. Cream the brown sugar and the softened butter and add the flour mixture to it. Add the oats and mix well.

In a separate bowl mix the cranberry sauce and sliced apples together. I like to place the apples in the cranberry sauce and mix it well to coat the apples. This prevents them from turning brown while you are completing the rest of the recipe. Pour the mixture into a 8 X 8 baking dish that has been sprayed with Pam. Spread the crisp topping over the mixture and bake until the topping is a toasty golden brown color and the mixture is hot throughout, about 45 minutes. It works wonderfully with Deep Fried Turkey, Cajun Corn and Dirty Rice. Imagine that!

Here's a tip: Like the Apple Crisp, it's good for breakfast, too.

This is absolutely one of my all time favorite side dishes made with some of my all time favorite ingredients. My Mom used to make this when we were youngsters for every special occasion meal that came around. It pairs well with Cajun Stuffed Pork Loin or Deep Fried Turkey and is easily complemented with other side dishes like Dirty Rice and Cajun Corn. I like a little more cinnamon and sugar than is called for here but I intentionally showed less to allow for you to season it to your taste. Because clove is a strong spice, be careful if you add more of that to the mixture. Do your taste testing before you add the beaten egg whites. Too much handling after the egg whites are added will cause the soufflé not to soufflé. If that happens just serve Sweet Potato Pudding!

2 cups cooked and mashed sweet potatoes
1 cup hot milk
½ teaspoon salt
1 tablespoon sugar
3 tablespoons butter
2 eggs, separated
1 teaspoon fresh ground nutmeg
1 teaspoon cinnamon
1/8 teaspoon ground clove
3/4 cup pecans (coarsely chop ½ cup
   of the pecans)
1 cup small marshmallows

Prep time: 30 min.
Cook time: 1½ hours in all
Yield: Approx. 8 servings

Line a cookie sheet with aluminum foil and bake the sweet potatoes until they are well done. When the potatoes are cool enough to handle peel and mash them and set aside. Scald the milk and dissolve the sugar and salt in it: add the butter and stir until melted. Add this mixture to the mashed potatoes and beat until light and fluffy. Separate the eggs, beat the yolks and add to the potatoes: add the nutmeg, cinnamon, clove and chopped pecans, and blend well. Beat the egg whites until stiff and fold lightly into the potato mixture along with half of the marshmallows. Pour into a buttered soufflé dish. If you don't have one, an ovenproof baking dish will work well but it should be deep enough to allow for the soufflé to rise. Quickly arrange the remaining marshmallows and whole pecans on the top and bake in a preheated 350° oven until the soufflé is set and the marshmallows are toasted delicately. Serve at once.

Mom's Sweet Potato Crunch

When Mom wasn't making Sweet Potato Soufflé as a side dish for Thanksgiving Dinner she made this great Sweet Potato Crunch. Just like the soufflé, I used to eat this like dessert. She was very fond of pecans and her original recipe carried a notation by the pecan entry that read, "More is good!"

3 cups cooked, mashed sweet potatoes
2 teaspoons cinnamon
¾ cup white sugar
½ teaspoon salt
2 eggs well beaten
½ stick melted butter
½ cup milk
½ teaspoon vanilla

Bake and mash the sweet potatoes as directed in the recipe for Sweet Potato Soufflé. Combine all of the ingredients in the bowl of a stand mixer and mix on medium speed until all ingredients are well combined. Spread the mixture in a suitable baking dish that has been sprayed with Pam. Add the topping.

Topping

1 cup brown sugar
½ cup flour
1 cup chopped pecans
1/3 cup melted butter

Prep time: 30 min.
Cook time: Approx. 2 hours in all
Yield: 10 servings

Combine all the ingredients and sprinkle over the sweet potato mixture. When the dish is baked the topping will spread. Bake for 30-50 minutes. Mom always liked hers baked a longer time to allow for the brown sugar topping and pecans to get a little bit crunchier. I can taste it now!

Celebration Catering truck and trailer

Good Times Are Getting Better

Desserts are an interesting item in our house. In the past we would go for long periods of time with dessert served only occasionally, mostly when we had guests. This is not because we don't like dessert; most times we just never get around to it. Later, when we started catering, we found that it was necessary to have desserts on the menu. It was then that we realized how many good dessert recipes we had. Once we got started with desserts for catered events, they just bled over into our regular meals at the house. They just did...that's my story and I'm sticking to it. There are some really great recipes in this section and we catered many of them with great success. I have included three recipes for sauces that go with some of the entries contained in this section. They are good enough to accompany many others as well, which is why I entered them as stand alone recipes.

Enjoy them; a lot of people certainly have.

Bread Pudding with Lemon Sauce and Chantilly Cream

Bread pudding is a particularly Southern commodity and many restaurants offer it as a standard dessert. Like most Louisiana dishes there are as many variations as there are folks cooking it. This is one that has worked particularly well for us. We borrowed heavily from Chef Paul Prudhomme's rendition of it in his first cookbook, Louisiana Kitchen. It was one of the first desserts that we included in our catering menu and it was our most successful. I can't even guess how much of this pudding we've made. It never fails to surprise people when they first taste it because of the marvelous blending of tastes. I'm always amazed that basic ingredients like these can produce such a result. At one catered event a very nice lady went into a sort of rapturous state after her first taste. After a few seconds she declared that it was, well, sensuous! Not everybody sees it that way, but it really is good.

3 large eggs
1 ¼ cups sugar
1 ½ teaspoons vanilla extract
1 ¼ teaspoons ground nutmeg
1 ¼ teaspoons ground cinnamon
¼ cup unsalted butter, melted
2 cups milk
5 cups cubed French bread, with crusts on

Prep time: 15 min.
Cook time: approx. 1 hr. in all
Yield: 8 servings

In the large bowl of an electric mixer, beat the eggs on high speed for three minutes until extremely frothy. Add the sugar, vanilla, nutmeg, cinnamon and butter and beat on high until well blended. Beat in the milk. Place the bread cubes in a large bowl and pour the egg mixture over them and toss until the bread is soaked. Let this mixture sit for about 30-45 minutes. Periodically pat the bread down into the mixture to keep it moist. Place in a pre-heated 350° oven and immediately lower the heat to 300°. Bake in loaf pan for 40 minutes and then increase the temperature to 425° and bake for an additional 15 to 20 minutes or until pudding is well browned and is starting to get crusty on top.

Serve the pudding by placing a couple of tablespoons of Lemon Sauce (see below) in the bottom of the bowl. Place the bread pudding on top of that and then top the pudding with a generous dollop of Chantilly Cream (see below).

When expanding this recipe be aware that the cook time is going to be lengthened. To test for doneness, I suggest inserting a table knife into the middle of the pudding. It is done when the knife comes out clean.

Bread Pudding with Lemon Sauce and Chantilly Cream

Lemon Sauce

This sauce can be prepared ahead of time and kept at room temperature.

2 tablespoons lemon juice
½ cup water
¼ cup sugar
2 teaspoons cornstarch, dissolved in ¼ cup water
1 teaspoon vanilla extract

Prep time: 15 min.
Cook time: 15 min.
Yield: 8 servings

Place the lemon juice, water and sugar in a 1-quart saucepan and bring to a boil. When the sugar is dissolved, stir in the cornstarch mixture and the vanilla. While stirring constantly cook the sauce over high heat until the mixture thickens and starts to bubble. Makes about ¾ cup.

Chantilly Cream

Food Lover's Companion describes Chantilly cream as a sweetened whipped cream often flavored with a liqueur. This one elevates that concept to a new level. It's sinfully delicious.

1 cup heavy cream
1½ teaspoons vanilla extract
1½ teaspoons brandy
1½ teaspoons Grand Marnier
3/8 cup sugar
1 tablespoon sour cream

Prep time: 15 min.
Yield: 8 servings

Chill a medium-sized bowl and the beaters of an electric mixer until very cold. Combine cream, vanilla, brandy, Grand Marnier in the bowl and beat with the electric mixer on medium for about 1 minute. Add the sugar and beat until it is well incorporated in the cream mixture. Add the sour cream and beat on medium until soft peaks form. This can be made ahead and held in the refrigerator. Makes approximately 1½ cups.

Old Fashioned Sweet Potato Pie

I used to love it when Mom made Sweet Potato Pie. She would make one for the family and one just for me. One pie didn't have a chance. Her pie was smooth and creamy with just the right amount of cinnamon, allspice and nutmeg. It's an easy pie to make and it holds well. To be honest, it was a long time before I found out how well it would hold because there was never any left to hold!

A word about sweet potatoes is probably in order here. Very often you will see "yams" on sale in grocery stores. From everything I've read on the subject sweet potatoes and yams are two different things. They are even from two different plant species. True "yams" are rarely grown and marketed in the United States! They are tropical. Sweet potatoes are commonly grown in the South. The issue gets confused because many growers, even in the South, very often market sweet potatoes as yams. I don't know how this got started but it is confusing. As an aside, you might be interested in knowing that the sweet potato is in the morning glory family! Does that explain the elementary school science experiment of growing a sweet potato vine?

3 eggs, slightly beaten
1 cup sugar
1 cup cooked, mashed sweet potatoes
1 cup half and half or evaporated milk
½ stick butter, melted
½ teaspoon allspice
½ teaspoon cinnamon
½ teaspoon nutmeg
pinch of salt

Prep time: 1½ hrs. in all
Cook time: Approx. 1 hour
Yield: 1 - 9" pie

Prepare the sweet potatoes as described in the recipe for Sweet Potato Soufflé found in *The Supporting Cast* section.

Combine the sugar, allspice, cinnamon, nutmeg, and salt and set aside. In the bowl of a stand mixer beat the eggs. While the beater is on set medium, add the sugar mixture, mashed sweet potatoes, milk and melted butter in sequence. When thoroughly blended pour batter into an uncooked pie shell and bake at 400° for 10 minutes. Reduce heat to 350° and bake for about 45 minutes or until a knife inserted in the center comes out clean.

Fudgy Brownies

We were always on the lookout for something new in the catering business. We didn't want people to think there was anything stale about our menu, so we worked hard at bringing new ideas out regularly. These brownies were one of those "innovations." Brandon found the recipe on the side of a 10-ounce package of Saco premium cocoa, changed the proportions a little to fit our needs and we were in business. We used to bake them up in a #3 cast iron skillet and serve them topped with ice cream as a dessert for two. If you like brownies, this is a grand slam! This recipe makes two #3 cast iron skillets of brownies or one 8" X 8" cake pan.

1 stick unsalted butter
½ cup Saco premium cocoa, if you can find it. Hershey's works if you can't.
1 cup sugar
2 eggs
1 teaspoon vanilla
½ cup flour
¼ teaspoon salt
½ cup chopped pecans

Prep time: 30 min.
Cook time: 25-30 min.
Yield: 16-2" square brownies

Preheat the oven to 350°. Lightly butter two #3 cast iron skillets or one 8" X 8" cake pan and set aside. In a medium saucepan melt the butter. When melted, remove from heat, add cocoa and stir until well blended. Add the sugar and mix well. Add the eggs, one at a time, and beat well. Stir in the vanilla, flour and salt. Do not overbeat. Fold in the chopped pecans. Divide and spread evenly in the two skillets or cook in one batch in a square cake pan. Bake 25-30 minutes until a toothpick inserted in the middle comes out clean. We found the cast iron skillet gave us a nice crusty edge. This recipe expands easily...it just depends on how big of a batch you want to stir up!

Grandmother Cook's Banana Pudding

We realized early on in the catering business that if we prepared the dishes we grew up eating, it would be very different from the food typically catered in this part of the world. I know there are exceptions to this, but most caterers around here don't cook; they open up cans of prepared food or thaw a frozen prepared product, warm them up and serve it. The same is true for desserts as it is for entrees. After preparing hundreds of servings of New Orleans Style Bread Pudding with Lemon Sauce and Chantilly Cream, a whole lot of Peach Cobbler or Apple Crisp and who knows how many Sweet Potato Pecan Pies, we started looking for another old standard to resurrect. This recipe filled the bill and it was a hit the first time we showcased it. This recipe has been around in Carol's family for a long time and is proven. All we did with it was make more of it! By the way, as proof that it expands well, we served a party of 100 the first time we made it. Since then it has been presented many times to groups as large as 300.

5-6 bananas, peeled and sliced
2 cups sugar
6 eggs, separated
4 tablespoons flour
2 teaspoons vanilla
2 tablespoons melted butter
2 cups milk
1 box vanilla wafers

Prep time: 30 min.
Cook & Assembly time: 40 min.
Yield: 15 generous servings

Whisk the sugar and flour together and set aside. Separate the eggs and set the whites aside. In the bowl of a stand mixer beat the egg yolks on medium speed. While the mixer is running on medium add the sugar and flour combination and blend thoroughly. With the mixer still running drizzle in the melted butter and milk and combine thoroughly. In a stainless steel or aluminum saucepan cook the mixture over medium heat, stirring constantly to prevent sticking. When the pudding thickens remove from the heat and add vanilla. Beat egg whites until stiff and fold into the pudding.

To assemble the pudding, layer a 9' X 13" deep dish with vanilla wafers. Next add a layer of bananas and then finally a layer of pudding. Repeat the layers until all pudding is used. Top with a final layer of vanilla wafers. This can be made ahead of time and held in the refrigerator until ready to serve.

Here's a tip: For a little variation I sprinkle fresh blueberries in each layer and add a shower of them on the top for color.

Grandmother Cook's Banana Pudding

Just for fun...to prepare this pudding for 300 requires approximately the following volume of ingredients:

23 pounds bananas
13 pounds sugar
7½ dozen eggs, separated
1¼ pounds flour
2/3 cup vanilla
1 pound butter
1 gallon milk
15 pounds vanilla wafers

Because of the volume it's also necessary to prepare it in 4 batches.

Cindi's Butter Rum Peach Topping

Carol and I were visiting Cindi and Bill Schubnel's home for dinner one evening and Cindi served this for dessert. She downplayed the recipe but it knocked me out of my chair! It's fast, easy and really good, so I stole the recipe! The rule of thumb on that subject is simple: Don't let me watch you cook it if you don't want the recipe to get out. This topping is quite versatile and will work in a number of recipes but it's great on plain vanilla ice cream.

5 large peaches, sliced
1 cup brown sugar
1 stick unsalted butter
2 ounces dark rum

Prep time: 15 min.
Cook time: 15 min.
Yield: 8 servings

Melt butter in a large skillet. Add brown sugar and rum and mix well. Add peaches and cook until soft. Serve over ice cream. It doesn't get much simpler than that.

Apple Crisp

Here is another favorite of ours that we used extensively in the catering business. The preparation is simple and it was a great hit for us when we served it. LaCrescent, Minnesota, located just across the Mississippi River from LaCrosse, Wisconsin, is home to many large apple orchards and the annual Applefest. When the apple harvest started we would feature this dessert. The freshness of the apples, the wonderful tastes of brown sugar, cinnamon and nutmeg, and the crispness of the topping are a real delight. Try it with a crisp, tart apple for best results. I tried using one of the handy peeler/slicers from Pampered Chef and found that the apple slices were too thin. They get mushy when cooked if sliced to thinly. I prefer to have the apple texture in this dessert. Also, I sized this recipe for eighteen servings because it's good for breakfast the next morning!

4 pounds apples, peeled, cored and
    sliced thinly
½ cup water
1 cup sugar
1 cup light brown sugar
1 teaspoon ground nutmeg
1 teaspoon cinnamon
½ teaspoon salt
1½ cups flour
1 cup butter

Prep time: 45 min.
Cook time: 1 hour
Yield: 18 servings

Preheat oven to 350°. Peel, core and slice the apples. Arrange the apples in a shallow baking dish. Sprinkle the water over the apples. In a separate bowl, combine the sugars, spices, salt and flour. Cut in the butter until the mixture is coarse and crumbly. Spoon the topping over the apples. Cover with foil and bake for 30 minutes. Uncover and bake 30 more minutes or until the topping is golden and crusty.

Incredibly Easy Fruit Cobbler

Believe me when I tell you that this is a quick and easy recipe that will delight your guests. I'll give you two versions of it and expand your fruit cobbler universe by the number of fresh fruits you care to try. This was the first dessert we used in the catering business and it was always popular. It expands easily. If memory serves me, the last time we made it in the catering business we did so for 100 people. Take that cue to mean that it expands easily. When making it at the house I always use a deep ten-inch cast iron skillet, otherwise know as a chicken fryer.

1 stick unsalted butter
1 large can sliced yellow cling peaches or any fruit you wish
1 cup flour
1 cup sugar
1 tablespoon baking powder
1 cup milk

Prep time: 15 min.
Cook time" 45 min.
Yield: 10 servings

Preheat the oven to 375°. Melt the butter in the skillet and swirl it around to coat the sides. You'll be glad you did when you start to clean up the skillet! Add the peaches with their juice and warm them up while you are mixing the batter. Whisk the flour, sugar and baking powder together and add the milk. Mix until all ingredients are well incorporated. Pour the batter in the middle of the melted butter and peaches and bake for 45 minutes. When done the batter will have risen to the top and will be a nice toasty golden brown. It is cakey in texture. Serve hot with ice cream or the Chantilly Cream from the Bread Pudding recipe and enjoy the accolades.

To use fresh fruit (I've used Door County cherries, blackberries, raspberries, apples, plums and peaches to name a few) just make a simple syrup with 1/3 cup sugar and ¾ cup water. Heat the water to dissolve the sugar. Add 3 cups of the fresh fruit and warm the fruit for about ten minutes. (You can even use a frozen berry mix that is available at most grocery stores as well. Treat it the same as you do fresh fruit.) To make the cobbler use this mixture in place of the large can of prepared fruit. Have some fun and experiment with this recipe.

Cheesecake

When we started the catering business, it seemed like everybody we talked to expected us to have a cheesecake on the menu. In keeping with our commitment to using our own recipes for everything we served, we needed to come up with a cheesecake recipe. Brandon went to work and did just that. The inspiration for this came from a professional chef's cookbook and has been modified for our use. This was a home run the first time out. The Butter Pecan Sauce and the Blueberries with Cream de Cassis found toward the end of this section make excellent toppings for this cheesecake.

1½ cups sugar (3/4 pound if you have a scale)
7 tablespoons cornstarch (2 ounces if you have a scale)
2½ pounds cream cheese (you do the math—it comes in 8 ounce bricks)
5 eggs
1 egg yolk
1 tablespoon vanilla extract
1 tablespoon lemon zest (zest from 1 lemon)
5 ounces heavy cream

Prep time: 30 min.
Cook time: Approx. 2 hrs. in all
Yield: 1–10 in. Cake

Press the graham cracker crust (see next page) firmly into an even layer in the prepared pan. Bake at 350° for about 7 minutes, or until golden brown. Remove the crust from the oven and set it aside to cool before adding the batter. Lower the oven setting to 300° when you remove the crust. Next sift together the sugar and cornstarch and set aside. Combine the eggs, egg yolk, vanilla, and lemon zest in a separate bowl and set aside.

Cream together the sugar and cornstarch mixture and the cream cheese in the bowl of a stand mixer. Using the paddle attachment, beat on medium speed until smooth. Add one fourth of the egg mixture at a time while the mixer is on medium speed. Fully incorporate each addition before adding the next. Scrape down the sides of the bowl after each addition. Add the heavy cream in a steady stream while the mixer is running on medium speed. Once again, scrape down the sides of the bowl as necessary. Carefully pour the mixture into the spring-form pan and bake in a water bath in a 300° oven until the center is set. Depending on your oven, this should take approximately 90 minutes. Check for doneness by inserting a cake tester in the center of the cake. It is done when the tester comes out clean. Refrigerate overnight. When sufficiently chilled the cake should separate from the sides of the pan. Carefully remove the spring band. This cake typically provides twelve servings.

Graham Cracker Crust

There is nothing exotic about this crust. It's just good and easy to make.

15 graham crackers, crushed into crumbs (8 ounces if you have a scale)
6 tablespoons sugar (3 ounces if you have a scale)
9 tablespoons butter, melted (4½ ounces if you have a scale)

Prep time: 10 min.
Cook time: 7-8 min
Yield: 1-10 inch crust

Preheat the oven to 350°. Coat a springform pan lightly with butter and line the bottom of it with parchment paper. Set aside.

You can buy graham crackers already crushed in the baking aisle of most large grocery stores. Otherwise you can pulse them in a blender or food processor. If none of that works crumble them in a large Ziploc bag and roll them with a rolling pin. The objective is to end up with fine crumbs. Blend the crumbs together with the sugar and add the melted butter. Stir the mixture well to incorporate all ingredients.

Mom's Oatmeal Cookies

Here's a classic. I remember eating these cookies when I was barely able to walk. Well, maybe I was a little bit older than that, but I know that I've enjoyed them for a long time. In recent years I've substituted dried cherries for the raisins with great success. There were several occasions in the catering business when we cooked for an all day business event. It was a breakfast, lunch, golf and dinner sort of thing. The client requested some cookies for after dinner and we pulled this recipe out, dusted it off and made thirty dozen or so of them. Folks were coming back and grabbing two or three at a time before they headed off to the golf course. Mom would have been proud.

1½ cups sifted flour
1 teaspoon soda
1/8 teaspoon salt
1 cup unsalted butter
2 eggs, beaten
1 cup sugar
1 cup brown sugar
1 teaspoon cinnamon
1 teaspoon vanilla
3 cups quick cooking oats
1½ cups raisins or dried cherries

Prep time: 30 min.
Cook time: Approx 6 min./.batch
Yield: ?

Preheat the oven to 400°. Sift the flour, soda, salt and cinnamon together and set aside. Beat the eggs and set aside. In the bowl of a stand mixer, using the paddle attachment, cream the sugars and butter until well blended and soft. Add the eggs and mix well. Add the sifted ingredients and mix well. Remove the bowl from the mixer and fold in the oats and raisins or dried cherries with a large serving spoon until all ingredients are incorporated into stiff dough. Using a standard serving spoon to scoop the dough out in golf ball sized portions, place the dough on a cookie sheet and bake for 6 minutes or until cookies are golden brown. When cooled the cookies should have crispy edges and should be somewhat chewy. I don't know how many it makes – depends on how big you make them. There are never any leftovers anyway.

Mom's Original Custard Sauce

I have always loved a good custard sauce. When we were growing up Mom would make this one on special occasions. One night in Lafayette, Louisiana I had an "envie" for a good custard sauce. That would be a craving, as the Cajuns would call it. I didn't have a recipe for custard sauce so I had to call Mom for a quick fix for the problem. She did as she always did when I called her for a recipe; she just started rattling it off. Just like that -- no looking at a recipe, no stopping to think about it -- just rattling it off. As it turns out this was my Grandmother's recipe so it's been around for a while. If you've never made custard sauce you really need a double boiler and a little patience. Special care should be taken when mixing the ingredients to make sure that it doesn't get lumpy. Lumps are a bad thing! The reason for the double boiler is to keep it from scorching. That's not good either. If you do get a few lumps in it you can always strain it and nobody will know the difference.

2 tablespoons sugar
1 tablespoon flour
1 dash salt
1 egg yolk, slightly beaten
1 ¼ cup milk
1 teaspoon vanilla

Prep time: 15 min.
Cook time: 30 min.
Yield: 8 servings

Slightly beat the egg yolk and add it to the milk in the double boiler. Whisk the sugar, flour and the salt together. Carefully add the dry ingredients to the milk and egg mixture while whisking it. This is the time when lumps will form if you're not careful. Cook over medium heat until thickened. It is necessary to stir this constantly. When the mixture is thickened, add the vanilla. This sauce is as good as it gets when ladled over bread pudding, blackberry cobbler or any of about a hundred other desserts. It doesn't expand very easily. It has taken me a long time to get good enough with this recipe to double it without it being too thin. I think a lot of it has to do with the double boiler.

Blueberries with Red Currant Jelly and Crème de Cassis

In the quest for interesting sauces and toppings here's one that takes center stage and it is one of my personal favorites. These blueberries literally burst with flavor when you bite down on them. Serve this sauce on top of good vanilla ice cream or as a topping on your favorite cheesecake. It will be a hit either way.

½ cup red currant jelly
1½ tablespoons crème de cassis
2 cups fresh blueberries, washed and drained

Prep time: 15 min.
Cook time: 1 min.
Yield: 8 servings

Heat the jelly in a glass measuring cup in the microwave until it melts, about 30 seconds. Stir in the crème de cassis. Place the blueberries in a large bowl and pour in the jelly mixture. Gently toss until the berries are coated. Refrigerate until ready to use.

Butter Pecan Sauce

I found this sauce printed on the back of a bag of brown sugar a long time ago. It's good on ice cream and is absolutely outstanding on Apple Crisp. We used to serve it warmed as a topping for cheesecake. It's not necessary to toast the pecan pieces but it does add a slight crunch to the mix and a shade of taste variation. Try it both ways and see which one you like best.

½ cup butter
1 cup toasted pecan pieces
1 cup firmly packed brown sugar
1/3 cup heavy cream
¼ cup corn syrup

Prep time: 15 min.
Cook time: 15 min.
Yield: 8 servings

In a heavy saucepan, melt the butter. Add the pecans and heat until the butter is lightly browned. Stir in the brown sugar, cream and corn syrup; cook gently until sugar is completely dissolved. Do not overcook. I find it best served warm.

Buz and Tim carving turkeys

Lagniappe

This is a Cajun term that, loosely translated, means "a little extra." If you understand the term "baker's dozen" you get the idea. Many times when you do business in South Louisiana the proprietor will give you a little extra to show appreciation for your business. It's a nice custom and I always thought it was a genuine gesture.

It applies here as well. I do appreciate having had the opportunity to share these stories and recipes with you, and have included a final section, a lagniappe, that has a few extra little tidbits, seasoning mixes and some various and sundry information Carol and I have gleaned from the past 40 years of cooking and entertaining. There are also a few recipes that just didn't fit anywhere in the book that I wanted to share. I hope you enjoy them.

Lagniappe

Celebration Seasonings Cajun Style
All Purpose Seasoning Blend

Since this spice blend has been mentioned many times in recipes throughout the book, it's only right that it should be included here. It was developed in my kitchen because I was unable to find any of several comparable products on the grocery store shelves in La-Crosse, Wisconsin when we moved here in 1989. Like everybody else in Louisiana, I had been using Tony's Creole Seasoning along with a couple of others that were also quite good. It was a hassle to have them shipped up here from Louisiana so I took matters into my own hands. After considerable experimentation I arrived at the final version of this mix in about 1993 and began making it as gifts for all of my friends. They loved it and had standing orders for more of it on record. When we started *Celebration Catering LLC* a lot of folks were interested in how we seasoned our food. Brandon and I did a little more research and eventually brought it to market in about 2001. It is blended and packed for us by Foran Spice Company in Milwaukee, Wisconsin under our proprietary recipe and we have sold quite a bit of it in a couple of grocery stores in LaCrosse and very often when we catered an event. It is now available at our favorite wine purveyor, The Wine Guyz in LaCrosse, Wisconsin. It truly is an all purpose blend and it works well on meats, in soups, gumbos and jambalayas, and even on vegetables. I'm just about as proud of this recipe as I am of Tim's Never Fail Lighter Than Air Buttermilk Biscuits developed way back in 1968!

2 ½ cups salt
½ cup chili powder
¼ cup granulated garlic
¼ cup sweet paprika
1/8 cup red pepper
1/8 cup black pepper
1/8 cup white pepper
1/8 cup hot paprika

Prep time: 15 minutes
Yield: 4 cups or approximately 28 ounces

Don't be put off by the number of peppers included in the recipe. If you taste it right out of the canister or the bowl in which you blend it, it is going to seem hot. When you cook with it, the chili powder, granulated garlic and sweet paprika go to work and the blend is not nearly as hot. In any case, most of the recipes call for you to season to taste. Try it out, you will like it. If you don't want to buy all of the ingredients, it is available through us. Also, if you mix your own, I suggest you use a sealed container to mix it in and, by all means, after you've mixed it up, resist the temptation to take a sniff of it until all the dust is settled in the container. To do so would be something like dropping that 12 pound frozen turkey into 3-4 gallons of hot peanut oil! There would be some kind of an explosion.

Creole Butter

A lot of folks like to cook a steak and then put a pat of butter on top of it after it's done. If you like that, then try it with this butter; it will knock your socks off! It is also great to sauté shrimp using this butter, and it works wonderfully with chicken breasts as well. I tried some of it on plain white rice and found it to be very interesting. You can halve this recipe easily or do what I do. Mix the whole batch and give half of it to a friend.

1 pound unsalted butter
2 tablespoons Worcestershire sauce
4 tablespoons garlic, finely minced
1 ½ teaspoons cayenne pepper
½ teaspoon fresh ground black pepper
½ teaspoon thyme
½ teaspoon oregano
½ teaspoon kosher salt
1 teaspoon crushed red pepper flakes

Prep Time: 15 minutes
Yield: Approximately 1¼ lbs.

In a mixer or food processor, mix all ingredients except the butter. Add the butter in chunks and mix until all ingredients are well incorporated. When butter chunks no longer appear in the mix, pack into a sealed container and refrigerate. It will last a couple of weeks in the refrigerator.

Garlic Mesquite Infused Oil

Several years ago somebody came out with a mesquite flavored oil in a spray can like Pam. We used it in the catering business when we served an appetizer tray of mesquite flavored grilled turkey tenderloins sliced thin with a party rye bread. The turkey was a great hit and was very easy to prepare. First we would spray it with the flavored oil, then season it with *Celebration Seasonings Cajun Style All Purpose Seasoning Blend* and refrigerate it overnight. When ready to cook all we did was cook the tenderloins on a hot grill and slice them. They were great. That mesquite flavored oil was also great on steaks, hamburgers, pork chops and chicken breasts. Now, you know what happened...whoever was making it quit making it! But it was too late; I was hooked. I did a little research on infused oils and decided I could make my own. Here's the recipe, which by the way reflects the addition of a little garlic juice that gives it a little more dimension.

½ cup light olive oil or Canola oil
1 teaspoon mesquite liquid smoke
1 teaspoon garlic juice

Prep time: 10 minutes
Yield: Approx. ½ cup

Mix the ingredients and pour them into one of those little pump up kitchen misters that you can buy at any good kitchen shop. When you're ready to use it, shake up the mister to blend all of the ingredients, pump it up and spray it on. Works great! If you like more or less mesquite or garlic flavor, simply adjust the amounts to your taste.

Fruit Dip

We received a lot of calls for a Fruit Tray when we were in the catering business. One item that gave us some trouble was an adequate fruit dip. We had used a couple of different ones and they were lackluster. Often times when we've encountered a problem while working together my friend Dan Thelen is fond of saying, "Let's just keep working and a solution will present itself." That's a neat approach and it works. That's exactly how this fruit dip problem was solved. One day this recipe just presented itself. That's it! The dip just showed up and it was great. It holds very well and goes well with any fruit.

15 ounces vanilla yogurt
1 cup Cool Whip
1 package vanilla instant pudding
½ cup drained crushed pineapple
1 cup light rum (optional)

Prep time: 15 minutes
Yield: 3 ½ - 4 cups

Mix the yogurt, cool whip and pudding together. Add the drained pineapple and the light rum. Served chilled with an array of fresh fruit. This mix holds well for two or three days in the refrigerator.

Cast Iron Cookware

I have been using cast iron cookware since I started cooking. Mom had several skillets and a large Dutch oven that she used for a lifetime, and I literally grew up watching her cook in cast iron cookware. When Carol and I got married my sister, Dianne, gave us a skillet and Jesse Mae Turner, who had worked for Carol's family forever, gave us a chicken fryer. We still use both regularly. Somewhere around 1983, shortly after my grandmother died at the age of 103, I was given several of her cast iron pieces by Mom and my Aunt Audrey. One of the skillets was reputed to be about 200 years old and, from the look of the patina on the old skillet, I wouldn't argue that point too much. That acquisition gave me a total of about 7 or 8 pieces of cast iron that looked great hanging on a wall in our kitchen. About then I really got interested in collecting more cast iron and began to haunt flea markets, garage sales and every old antique/collectible shop I had a chance to visit. Over the years Carol and I have passed on the tradition by giving a cast iron skillet away as wedding gifts. Packaged with a dry mix for Mom's Cornbread and a copy of the recipe, a good cast iron skillet makes quite a unique and useful gift. It's also a good bet one of these gifts will last a lifetime.

These days it would take several pages to list all of the various pieces I have and use. There are Dutch ovens from about a 3-quart size all the way up to a 6½-gallon "Class A" jambalaya-cooking behemoth. Then we get into the big stuff, an 11-gallon cauldron and a 9-gallon ham boiler complete with a custom made lid provided by my good friend Dan Thelen. Skillets range from a #3 all the way up to a #14 and include a couple of different styles of square ones. The collection also has a good representation of griddles, muffin pans, cornbread cookers and a couple of serious roasters.

It's interesting to note that from colonial times all the way to the current day, cast iron cooking utensils have been designed and manu-factured to meet just about every need. It's also amazing that if any piece of cast iron has been reasonably cared for, or at the very least not left exposed to the elements so that it rusts, it can be refurbished to look like almost new and thereby gain a new lease on a cooking life.

On a trip to Louisiana, Carol and I stopped at an old antique store in Southern Missouri. I bought two pieces of the heaviest cast iron that I have ever seen. When I was checking out, the proprietor and I got into a discussion about the restoration of cast iron. He told me that an elderly gentleman in town had refurbished a lot of it over the years and he showed me several examples of his work. I was amazed when he told me the secret. The old man used a large vat of water in which he had dissolved a can of Drano. He immersed the piece of cast iron in it and left it submerged for about a week or so, depending on how much carbon build-up it had on it. That's all he knew and I was left to my own devices to figure out the rest of the process. Here's what I discovered would work. The lye in the Drano dissolves the carbon build-up on the piece and most often all that is necessary to finish cleaning it is to burnish it with a fine wire brush. After washing the piece thoroughly to remove the lye and the residue from the burnishing step, the next step is to dry it very well. Finally the piece is seasoned with a coating of oil and is heated to approximately 500° F for about an hour. (Here's a tip: I prefer to use shortening rather than cooking oil because it doesn't get as sticky. I also prefer to do this step on a grill outside because of the smoke it generates.) The process is not difficult and after refurbishing dozens of pieces I can attest to the success of the method. I once talked a lady at a flea market into selling me a skillet for $1.00 because it was so caked with carbon we couldn't even read the markings on the bottom. After about two weeks soaking in the lye it transformed into a #9 Griswold skillet worth about $50.00 that is hanging on the wall today!

The heat transfer and retention properties of cast iron are excellent. If you are not familiar with the cookware it's worth taking the time to understand how to properly use and care for it. For openers you should know that some foods, like sautéed mushrooms, turn black when cooked in cast iron and look unappetizing. For those foods there are many other types of cookware that will work just fine. However, if you want to sear a steak or fry a hamburger or cook just about anything that requires high heat or long cooking times with low heat, there is nothing better than cast iron. If anything should stick to the skillet or pot, heat it up and pour water in it. Let it simmer for a few minutes and scrape it with a spatula. Then move to the sink and use a stiff bristle brush and run hot water in the utensil while brushing it vigorously. When it's clean, place the skillet or pot on a lit burner and let it get very hot. Dry it well with a couple of paper towels. When it cools to the point where it can be handled, spray Pam all around the inside and let it sit for a few minutes. Wipe it well with a paper towel to remove the excess oil and store it. All of that may sound like a hassle but when you consider that you will never have to throw it away because you wore the non-stick surface off of it or because it overheated and warped, it's not such a bad trade off. The real bonus is that it only gets better with use. The clean up takes less and less time and the finish takes on a rich black patina that tells its own tale of many well-prepared meals.

Common Conversions

Because of the necessity to expand and convert recipes in the catering business I discovered that there is quite a bit of what I call "kitchen math." When we started I never thought the situation would evolve to the point that it was necessary to have a calculator and a scale in the kitchen, but it quickly did. Early on, Brandon started using weights when cooking larger volumes and I, being the old dog learning new tricks, adapted later. In the interest of time, along the way, we compiled this list of commonly used conversions. It is by no means inclusive but it contains the measurements we used the most. It proved to be a great timesaver. You will notice that the dry measures are converted to weights. Additionally, if you have a scale that allows you to change from ounces to the metric scale, that scale is more accurate for the lighter weight ingredients. The idea in expanding a recipe is to obtain consistent results and the dry weights will help you do that. Just for drill, try converting *Tim's Incomparable Buttermilk Pancakes* to make about 500 pancakes and you'll see what I mean. I hope you find this list as useful as we did.

1 cup flour ------------------------------------- 5 ounces
1 cup sugar ----------------------------------- 7.2 ounces
1 cup cornmeal------------------------------- 5.7 ounces
1 cup rice --------------------------------------- 7 ounces
1 tablespoon baking powder ------------------.5 ounces
1 tablespoon sugar-----------------------------.5 ounces
1 teaspoon Celebration Seasoning ------------ 5 grams
1 tablespoon shortening -----------------------.4 ounces
1 tablespoon butter ---------------------------- 5 ounces
8 tablespoons butter ------- ¼ pound =1/2 cup=1 stick
16 tablespoons butter------- ½ pound =1 cup =2 sticks
32 tablespoons butter ----- 1 pound =2 cups =4 sticks

3 teaspoons =1 tablespoon
4 tablespoons =1/4 cup = 2 fluid ounces
5 1/3 tablespoons =1/3 cup = 2 2/3 fluid ounces
8 tablespoons = ½ cup = 4 fluid ounces
16 tablespoons =1 cup = 8 fluid ounces
1 cup = ½ pint
2 cups = 1 pint = 16 fluid ounces
2 cups = 1 quart = 32 fluid ounces
4 quarts = 1 gallon = 128 fluid ounces

1 cup raw rice = 3 cups cooked rice
8 ounces uncooked spaghetti = 4 cups cooked
4 ounces cheese = 1 cup shredded
1 pound cheese = 4 cups shredded
1 teaspoon dried herbs = 1 tablespoon fresh herbs
1 clove garlic = ½ teaspoon

Glossary

Alexandria, Louisiana The city where I grew up. It is located some-what in the geographic center of the state and is known as the Hub City or Cenla (an amalgam of Central La.)

Andouille   [ahn doo ee] A smoked spicy Cajun sausage said to have its origins in the Alsace region of France. Many people from that region settled in Louisiana along the Mississippi in an area known as the German Coast.

Avoyelles Parish The northernmost of the Cajun parishes. Some of my maternal ancestors migrated from the Alsace region of France to New Orleans and then to Marksville, Louisiana, the parish seat of Avoyelles Parish.

Baton Rouge, Louisiana   The capitol of Louisiana. Carol and I lived in Baton Rouge on three different occasions.

beignet A traditional New Orleans style risen doughnut served hot, dusted with confectioner's sugar and served with café au lait. It is derived from the French word for "fritter."

boudin   [boo dan] Considered a delicacy in South Louisiana. A well seasoned sausage typically made with pork, rice and onions; however, there are some fine examples of seafood based boudin. The term is French for "pudding." A pound of boudin and a six-pack of Budweiser are considered by many Cajuns to be a 7-course meal.

café au lait An elixir of note consisting of coffee and scalded milk. Best made with coffee laced with chicory. Check out the recipe for Cush-Cush and Café au Lait.

Cajun A corruption of the word Acadian. Although it is a complex story, suffice it to say here, the Acadians migrated from the maritime provinc-es of Canada around what is now known as Nova Scotia to the bayous of South Louisiana. Dr. Carl Brasseaux, a noted Louisiana historian, has done exhaustive research and has written extensively about the Cajuns. Their origins are in central France where they were primarily farmers. Their fare was simple and sturdy. When they came to the Loui-siana bayous west of New Orleans, they adapted their cuisine to use what was available. Many of their recipes are commonly know as "one pot meals." Some of my maternal ancestors also migrated from Acadia.

Celebration Catering LLC An outstanding example of a caterer that specialized in Louisiana cuisine.

Celebration Seasonings Cajun Style All Purpose Seasoning Blend A multipurpose seasoning blend developed by an outstanding caterer.

cher [shā] A Cajun corruption of the French word "chere" which means "dear." The common usage of the term as often means "friend" as it does "dear." A common greeting in South Louisiana might be *Comme ca va, cher?* (*How's it going, dear or (friend)?*) The answer would be something like *Ca va bien, et tu?* (*It's going well, and with you?*)

court-bouillon [coor bwe yawn] Translated literally means "short soup." In classic French cuisine it is a lightly flavored broth used to poach fish. In South Louisiana the broth is typically tomato based and well seasoned with a roux added. The fish is then cooked in the broth and both are served over rice.

crawfish A freshwater crustacean that looks like a little lobster, but that's as far as it goes. It has a distinct flavor that is prized in South Louisiana. Breaux Bridge, Louisiana, located in the Atchafalaya River Basin, is known as the Crawfish Capital of the World and the little town hosts the well known annual Crawfish Festival.

etouffee A popular dish made with crawfish. The delicacy is cooked in a butter sauce seasoned with celery, bell pepper and onion. It is typically served over rice. Etouffee means "to smother."

Creole There have been whole books written about this term. It is used most often in and around New Orleans and in South Louisiana. It is commonly used in reference to matters pertaining to cuisine; however, much has been written about the Creoles as an ethnic group. I would again defer to Dr. Carl Brasseaux on that subject. As it pertains to food, it usually refers to the evolution of cuisine in New Orleans. As a result of influences from those who ruled and settled the area, the cuisine of New Orleans is distinctive. The French, Spanish, Italians, Germans, Carribean islanders, African slaves and Native Americans all contributed much to the development of the foods so identified with the locale. Today the Cajun and Creole cuisines have fused to the point that some chefs refer to the combination simply as "Louisiana cuisine."

dirty rice There are folks in Louisiana that lay awake nights thinking about different ways to cook food and different names for what they cook. Thank God they are there, but they've got to get a little more dialed in than "dirty rice." When I first moved to LaCrosse, Wisconsin, it was hard enough to get some people to eat rice dressing let alone "dirty rice."

envie [ahn vie] A Cajun slang term meaning a "craving". Hey cher, it's 70 degrees outside. With a "cool snap" like that I've got an envie for some gumbo!"

French Market, The An historic open air market located along the Mississippi River in the French Quarter of New Orleans.

gumbo A thick stew like soup served over cooked white rice that is a mainstay in the Cajun cook's repertoire. It can, and does, contain many different ingredients which vary depending on who's cooking and where you are in the state. You should be aware that everybody in South Louisiana eats gumbo and is more than willing to share with you the "proper" way to prepare it and the appropriate ingredients to include in it. Many folks even claim to have been weaned on it, which may not be too farfetched when you consider my daughter was eating chicken and sausage gumbo for lunch at a day care operated by Mrs. DeMarie in Lake Charles, Louisiana when she was 18 months old! See the recipe included in The Warm Up section of this book and you will find my version of gumbo which may, or may not, bear any resemblance to what some other "expert" calls gumbo.

hot Cajun food A gross misconception, perpetuated by the unknowing masses. Traditional Cajun food is not inherently too hot! Hot is a matter of personal taste for which this recipe book makes allowances, usually by the tag line "Season to taste"!

jambalaya A rice-based one pot meal, jambalaya is thought by many to be a derivative of Spanish paella. It is typically cooked with chicken, sausage and pork or any combination of the three. Many times shrimp is included depending on the cook and the region of the state. Most recently some innovative cooks have begun to substitute spaghetti for the rice, which naturally results in a dish called, what else, "pastalaya."

Lafayette, Louisiana Located in the heart of Cajun country this city is considered the capital of Acadiana (an amalgamated term coined by a local TV station in Lafayette many years ago when referring to the section of Louisiana settled by the Acadians).

mise en place   French term meaning everything in its place…refers to the process of organizing and pre-measuring all ingredients…a very useful technique.

parish   A governmental division that is the same as a county. The term is a holdover from the Napoleonic Code of Law which is still practiced in Louisiana (more or less). There are 64 parishes in Louisiana and by a House Concurrent Resolution passed in 1971, 22 of them have been officially recognized as Acadiana, the Cajun homeland originally settled by the Acadians.

red beans and rice   Thank God for the old time housewives in New Orleans that did the wash on Monday because without them we probably never would have figured out this recipe.

remoulade   A white sauce with a mayonnaise base served with chilled seafood. Think of it as a jazzed up tartar sauce.

roux   A base of browned flour and oil. See the included recipe. It is considered by many to be the linchpin in Cajun cuisine. My high school plane geometry teacher, Brother Max, considered The Pythagorean Theorem to be what he called the "pons assinorum" (his Latin term for "the bridge of asses"). Brother Max held that if you didn't understand that theorem you could not learn the rest of plane geometry. The same principle applies to a roux. By the way, I did cross that bridge under his tutelage but I certainly don't remember it now.

Southern Fried Chicken   A divinely inspired recipe for how to cook a humble fowl. That recipe was handed down long before the one for fried turkey, which, of course, received some heavenly guidance.

Index

D

E

F

G

H

T

U

V

W

To Order Copies of

Laissez les Bon Temps Rouler

ISBN 978-1-59879-326-8

You may order on line at:

www.AuthorsToBelieveIn.com

by phone at:

877-843-1007